Breaking Records

21 Lessons from 21 World Record Attempts

David W. Rush

ISBN: 9798638515058

DEDICATION

This book is dedicated to my loving and supporting wife, Jennifer Rush, and our two boys, Jeremy and Peter. A life lived with love is the most meaningful life there is. A life lived with the support I have had from you fills me with gratitude beyond words.

CONTENTS

ACKNOWLEDGMENTS

Thank you to all who helped make these records and this book possible.
Jennifer, thank you for the hours I needed to not only write the book but also practice for and break the records. Also thank you for the space I needed for all the supplies and practice in our living room, garage, kitchen, and yard. Thank you also for your gift of time taking photos, running cameras, holding stopwatches, and encouraging me when things didn't go my way. Thank you to Jeremy and Peter who are my biggest cheerleaders and practice partners. I'll "guggle" for and with you forever.

I also wanted to extend many thanks to all those who have helped and supported me in my record attempts. Without your support, this could not have happened. Thank you to Mike and Becky Beacham, Michael Gilmore, Chris Gunning, Scott Smith, Jon Heggen, Jack Ward, Mike and Linda Rush, Daniel and Audrey Rush, Jonathan and Courtney Rush, Jonathan and Lisa Marie Hannon, Isaac Barrett, Pam Atkins, Angela Hemmingway and the Idaho STEM Action Center, Laurie Anderson and the Micron Foundation, Dr. Bob Kustra, Dr. Amy Moll, Dr. Kent Neupert, Leandra Aburusa-Lete and Boise State University, Don Bossi and FIRST, Dan and Andrea Hubbard, Josh and Megan Hamilton, Steve and Michelle Darden, Phil and Ashlee Chaffee, Rodd Ritchie, Brian Grant, Jeremy and Beka Cramer, Josh Cramer, Jackson Cramer, Steve Sommers, and so many more at Cole Community Church, Kirsten Holmes and the Idaho Speakers Bureau, Arthur Lewbel, Cole Perkinson and the MIT Juggling Club, Mike and Michelle Bost, Ashlie Brown and others at MIT, Matt Freeman, Dave Hill, and the Idaho State Board of Education, Michael Whitty, Paul O'Neill and GUINNESS WORLD RECORDs, Troy Rainville, Amy Wilson and Science North, Beth Woods, Alex Hartman and the Ada Community Libraries, Jacob Post and the Oak Brook Public Library, Aaron Olswanger and Boise High School, John Doherty, Bryan and Capital High School, Jon Watson and Centennial High School, the TODAY show, the Huckabee show, America's Got Talent, and The Bob and Tom Show. Thank you also to Jack Ulrich who encouraged me to write this book.

Thank you to my coworkers at Cradlepoint whose support has been invaluable including Paul Rodeghiero, Chris Knight, George Mulhern, Val Heusinveld, Jodi Richter, Sadie Hanigan, Michelle Carskaddon, Jessica Christie, Michelle Obrochta, Jake Smith, Mike Hagman, Mauricio Steffen, Ian Pennell, Marc Bresniker, Ryan Adamson, Joe Wagner, Keith Travis, Matt Knollenberg, Stoney Tuckness, Aparnika Naveen, Terrese Donnelly, Jake Alger, Matt Messenger, Ken Hosac, Kevin Hercules, Matthew Thueson, Alden Miljkovic, Kelly Hendricks, Bryan Passmore, Matthew Razutis, Kenji Hyde, Mitch Meade, Ethan Lewis, Jen Pulsifer, Laura Wylde, Summer Visser, Patrick Harper, Kevin Everett, Carrie Cate-Clements, Kalyan Subramanian, Steven Johnson, Steve Johnson, Steven Connelly, Joe Colapietro, Chris and Estee Woods, Carl Altman, Chris LaPeters, Chris Rorris, Dan Gregory, Daniel Dubief, David Earp, David Koby, Edwin Mendoza, Jake Montaba, Jen Phillips-Garcia, Jim Farquharson, Keith Plaskett, Ken Tucker, Kevin Johnson, Lee Brumagin, Michael Dickens, Ray Clounch, Scott Mench, Stephen Byrum, Vince Cedillo, Bill Hunt, Dave Beilke, Venessa Sierra, Andy Hawk, Kory Harker, Aron Talwar, Matt Andrews, Bryan Wood, Jeff Hubble, Ben Miller, Steve Wood, David and Alecia Murray, Presley Troyer, and more.

Thank you to my early readers including Mike Rush, Patricia Pierose, Becky Beacham, Andrea Hubbard, Jacob Green, Jennifer Rush, and others who helped make this debut book so much better than it would have been otherwise.

PROLOGUE

I didn't set out to become the fastest juggler in the world. Most people don't know what slow juggling is, but I have the record for that too. Juggling blindfolded was a gimmick I did for friends, but I have now juggled blindfolded longer than anyone in recorded history. I balanced large and precarious objects on my chin for fun, but never realized I could break a world record using a ladder, pool cue, lawnmower, chainsaw, or a bicycle. How then have I been able to break over 150 records? While breaking these world records and others, I've learned guiding principles that lead to achieving goals and finding success. I've learned what it means to have a growth mindset. I've developed grit and pushed myself past the artificial limits placed on myself by myself and others. My self-imposed limits were subconscious, but held me back, nonetheless.

I have attempted and broken more than 150 world records. While most have been successful, some have been spectacular failures. I learned much more from the failures than from the successes, because failure is the essence of learning. Failure provides an opportunity to improve. But failure hurts. Our natural reaction is to avoid putting ourselves in a situation where we could fail again, but that's the opposite of what we should do if we want to grow.

I learned that luck is when preparation meets opportunity. I learned that believing in myself dramatically increases the effectiveness of my practice, the likelihood I'll persevere, and my chances of success. I learned that focused, determined, unwavering, and continuous pursuit of a goal leads to success more often than not, even if success looks different than initially imagined. I also found that support from a network of family, friends, acquaintances, and like-minded people helped me overcome many of the challenges I faced along the way. I learned all these lessons and more while training for and attempting more than 150 world records. Best of all, I learned these lessons apply to many situations or to anyone who is trying to better themselves in pursuit of a goal.

1
GETTING STARTED IS HALF THE BATTLE

Fastest 800 Meters Joggling - 3 Objects
Previous Record: 2 minutes 13 seconds

When people hear I've broken over 150 Guinness World Records titles, most for juggling, balancing, or running, there's often an assumption that I'm a naturally gifted athlete. I'm not. I'm 35 years old, and on my 30th birthday, I didn't hold a single Guinness World Records title. What changed? How did I start breaking records? Did I suddenly go through some transformation that made it possible?

I grew up thinking I wasn't much of an athlete. My older brother beat me at every sport we ever played. He was only a year older than me, and although I was taller, he was the physically gifted one. He was the second-fastest sixth-grader in the city of Boise in the hundred-meter dash (by just a hair. To this day, my mom still thinks he won that final, hand-timed race.) He broke the seventh-grade mile running record at our junior high at 5 minutes, 26 seconds, and may have held it until the school was torn down two decades later. He also won the city wrestling tournament in ninth grade. With sculpted biceps, he was voted "best arms" for his ninth-grade yearbook without ever having lifted weights. He was the one recruited to the club soccer teams and who made the football coach angry when he decided not to pursue football.

I wasn't unathletic, but in comparison to my brother, it sure felt that way. It turns out, I was somewhere in the middle of the pack for athletic ability. I was picked last for two-hand touch football at recess in elementary school when I was playing with the most athletic kids, but when I was playing with the less coordinated bunch, I was often a top pick and sometimes even got to play quarterback. I often placed first or second in the sixth-grade shot put in the multi-school meets, but when it came time for districts, I wasn't even in the top 20. In ninth grade, I ran a 5-minute, 28-second mile which was fast enough to qualify for the district junior high meet. It was cool but not as impressive as it sounds since the best ninth-grade runners competed at the high school meets leaving a weakened field at my meets.

I was fascinated with Guinness World Records as a kid. I read the books, soaked in the pictures, and caught the Guinness World Records specials on television. I imagined myself as the people I saw in the books and on the show setting a Guinness World Records title. I even looked for records that seemed feasible and practiced the ones I could. After watching the record for most pint glasses balanced on the chin on a TV special, I took a 12-foot-long empty cardboard tube from a carpet roll out to the front yard and tried to balance it on my chin. I spent a significant amount of time practicing, imaging myself on TV breaking a record, but I never got good enough to keep it balanced for more than a few seconds. I was trying, but when I realized that my roll of cardboard weighed a lot less than a big stack of glasses and I wasn't even close to mimicking the record with my prop, I gave up. I eventually gave up on my dream of ever breaking a Guinness World Records title.

Until I changed my mind.

What was keeping me from breaking a record? As a child, I had been told that I could accomplish anything I wanted if I put my mind to it and worked hard. When I was an adult, I decided to test that aphorism. I tentatively broached the topic with my dad when I was 29. I wanted to promote STEM (science, engineering, technology, and math) education and I wanted to set a Guinness World Records title to do it. The only questions were, which record, and could I do it?

I got into joggling (a portmanteau of jogging and juggling) my senior year at MIT. I didn't consciously plan my entry into the niche sport of running while juggling. The only running I did was on a sports field. I played on about 40 intramural sports teams over my four years at MIT, including soccer, football, ultimate frisbee, softball, and unihoc. (Imagine playing field hockey on a basketball court with ice hockey walls while holding a 3-foot-long plastic hockey stick played with a whiffle ball and tiny little goals. It is a fun, fast, ridiculous-looking game.)

In the fall of 2006, my oldest brother Daniel invited my other brother Jonathan and me to Seattle for Thanksgiving. After I accepted the invitation and bought my plane ticket, he told me that he was running the Seattle Half Marathon that weekend along with his girlfriend (and now wife) Audrey. Jonathan and his wife Courtney also decided to run. We were competitive as kids, and I hadn't outgrown that, so I unwisely decided to pay the entry fee and run the half marathon as well. But why just run it? I had a friend at Harvard Divinity School, Zach Warren, who had recently set the Guinness World Records title for the fastest marathon run while juggling, and I decided that if I were going to run, I should try it while juggling (but not for a record). I laced up my cheap, worn-out tennis shoes, grabbed my juggling balls, and tried joggling for the first time. I ran five miles on my first training run and found that joggling came more naturally than I expected. I only dropped the balls a few times. The next run around the Boston bridge loop system was 7 miles, and I had even fewer drops. Those were my first two, and only two, training runs.

It was uncharacteristically cold that Thanksgiving weekend in Seattle which included a snow flurry that left the ground white. On the morning of the half marathon, it was frigid. I had never practiced juggling in the cold or with gloves and was too afraid to wear gloves that morning. For the first three miles of the race, my fingers were so cold that every time a ball landed in my hand, it felt like I was being stabbed by tiny, painful icicles. I considered giving up as tears of pain filled my eyes, but I had told too many people I was going to run the half marathon while juggling. The fear of shame was more powerful than the physical pain. I kept juggling as I ran. About three miles in, as my core body temperature increased, I felt the warmth spread slowly down my arms and into my hands. The needle stabs faded and eventually the juggling balls hitting my hands no longer caused pain. I ran 13.1 miles with only three dropped balls.

Unfortunately, two of the drops came at bad times. At the start of the race, I had my brothers Jonathan and Daniel, and wife and future wife, Courtney, and Audrey form a V-formation in front of me so the jostling crowd at the start wouldn't interfere with juggling. The first drop didn't come until several miles in and didn't cause a problem. The second drop was about 12 miles into the race running down a long slope in notoriously hilly Seattle. I dropped a ball and was so tired my stop was rather abrupt. There was another runner right behind me coming down the hill. The combination of his momentum with my unexpected stop resulted in a collision. Fortunately, neither of us was hurt, but I learned my lesson to never stop abruptly to pick up a ball without checking behind me first. The third and last drop was running into the stadium with hundreds of cheering fans, just a few dozen yards from the finish. I suspect folks who saw that drop assumed I didn't juggle the whole way. I finished the half marathon in 1 hour and 47 minutes, and juggling would forever be part of my running routine.

In mid-2014, as I searched for a Guinness World Records title to break, I became fascinated with the record for the fastest mile run while juggling. I had already joggled a couple more half marathons in the intervening years and had taken up running regularly in early 2013. In January of 2014, I ran the Walt Disney World Marathon. I completed the 26.2-mile course juggling every step of the way. I had plenty of base mileage from running during lunch with coworkers from Cradlepoint where I worked as a Product Manager.

It was time to take my training to the next level. I had a goal: I wanted to break the Guinness World Records title for the fastest mile while juggling. The record was 4 minutes, 42 seconds. I pursued it with a passion. I ran 4-6 days per week alternating between middle distance (5-7 miles), time trials (400m to 5k), intervals, hill runs, and recovery runs. The interval training was the hardest. I would run 100-meter sprint repeats, 200-meter sprint repeats, and 400-meter sprint repeats. I would alternate between them. I would run so hard that I'd keel over, heaving for air, with fire in my lungs and my legs burning. I wasn't going to use pain, my exercise-induced asthma, or any other ailment as an excuse to quit. I'd take a few moments to catch my breath and begin the next sprint. After a few months, my times improved, but not enough. While juggling, I could now beat my junior high mile record time of 5 minutes, 28 seconds, and even my all-time personal record set during college of 5 minutes, 23 seconds, but I felt 4 minutes 42 seconds might be unreachable.

Sometimes, in the quest for a goal, you will need to adjust your strategies and work smarter. My goal was to break a Guinness World

Records title. Choosing which record to break was an important part of the strategy. I decided to check all the joggling speed records from 100 meters to a full marathon. The 100-meter dash was an absurdly fast 11.68 seconds, and my friend's marathon record had been surpassed by Michal Kapral with a time of 2 hours, 50 minutes 12 seconds. I ran the time and distance conversions and confirmed what I had suspected after reviewing all the distance joggling record times: the 800-meter distance joggling record of 2 minutes, 13 seconds was the weakest. It also wasn't a previously recognized Guinness World Records title distance, but it was recognized by the juggling community, and Guinness World Records would use that time as the minimum mark to beat.

It was time to create my Guinness World Records account. It's a relatively straightforward process. I browsed to www.guinnessworldrecords.com and set up a free account. I put in my email address, created a password, and gave them my name. They also asked for my address and contact information (to contact me if necessary or mail a certificate if I set a record). On September 25, 2014, I submitted my first Guinness World Record application for "Fastest 800 m joggling with three objects – male." A month and a half later, on November 6, 2014, the application was accepted. I forwarded my wife the email with a one-line message: "Time to get serious!" Two minutes and thirteen seconds isn't very long, but it felt like it might take an eternity to reach it.

My best 800-meter time while juggling was 2 minutes 21 seconds. My 400-meter time while juggling was a crisp 1 minute 3 seconds. Trying to shave off those last 8 seconds in the 800-meter run seemed so tantalizingly close, and yet so far away. One thing about competition is that the adrenaline makes pushing through pain much easier. A time trial at the track with just me running and my wife timing was not representative of my performance capabilities (or so I hoped). I continued to train. I continued to push. I visualized the goal (breaking a Guinness World Records title), the prize (being a Guinness World Records title holder), and the glory in which I would bask. (I vastly overestimated the amount of glory breaking a Guinness World Records title would bring which turned out to be extremely helpful in my training). I pushed through the pain, the agony, and the countless times my head told me to give up: "skip today," "your body hurts," or "it's not worth it." If I could just get close enough, I knew the adrenaline in the moment would allow me to shave off the last couple of seconds.

After two and a half years of training, on August 27, 2015, I went on one last juggling run. I used a phone app with GPS called RunKeeper to track my runs and would manually input treadmill distances (usually on 1% grade since 0% is easier than running outdoors). Since starting in February of 2013, I had logged over 300 training runs. I had covered more than 2,000 miles. I had lost 25 pounds starting from 197 pounds on a nearly 6-foot 2-inch frame with a decent muscle base. I wasn't bulky to start, but now I was lean. I had fought through several injuries to my Achilles, tight calves, and IT-band issues that led to knee pain. I had faced the demons, and I kept pushing through. On this day, August 27, 2015, I went on what would have been another unremarkable run while juggling the 3 balls that had accompanied me for over 2,000 miles. Except on this day, I hurt my knee.

I didn't think much of it when it happened. It didn't feel too bad. It was less painful than many minor injuries I'd experienced before. But this time, it didn't get better. I took a few light runs to test my knee over the coming days but needed to take a day off. A day became a week, a week became a month, a month became several months. I went to a doctor and got x-rays taken. I went to another doctor and got an MRI. The results were inconclusive. I stretched, rolled, strengthened, and rested my knee. I got a second opinion. My knee wasn't getting better. I tried to push through the pain, but I couldn't. I felt like I was doing permanent damage to my knee every time I ran. I had to stop.

I had spent two years training for a singular goal, and I couldn't even attempt the record. I was frustrated. I found myself bordering on despair. But I fought back.

I had started this journey, and I wasn't about to give up. We all have dreams and goals, and sometimes the hardest part of reaching them is getting started. I had started, and while I was down, I certainly wasn't out. It was time to take this pause in training and view it as time freed up to focus on setting a different Guinness World Records title.

Fastest 800 Meters Joggling
Previous Record: 2 minutes 13 seconds
My Result: Did not attempt
Best time trial before injury: 2 minutes 21 seconds

2
RESILIENCE IS MORE THAN A VIRTUE

Longest Duration Blindfolded Juggling (3 Balls)
Previous Record: 6 minutes 29 seconds

In her book, *Grit: The Power of Passion and Perseverance*, Angela Duckworth makes a case that it's not talent, genius, or natural ability that most accurately predicts future success. She claims that grit is a better predictor of many, if not most, triumphs. How does someone bounce back from failure? How do they respond to adversity? What happens when they're asked to do something they cannot currently do or even imagine doing? Trying to predict the likelihood of reaching the pinnacle of an occupation is not easy. Examples of hard-to-predict successes, even for those already on the verge of success, include completing the Green Beret's notoriously difficult training, breaking into a top professional sport, becoming a successful entrepreneur, or reaching the peak of a musical profession. But even trying to predict common successes is not as straightforward as it seems. The questions: will a student graduate high school, a candidate will become a productive employee, or a person complete a goal aren't easy answers to predict. Natural talent, SAT scores, prodigy status, a promising start, good grades, or past success are not guarantors of success. Even more surprising is that they're often not (or only weakly) correlated with future success. Grit is. Grit predicts success, more than talent, genius, or natural ability.

People with grit don't dwell on failure. They don't let the fear of not completing a task stop them from starting. They respond to adversity by stepping up and pushing through. When confronted with a task they don't know how to do, they jump right in and get to work, even though the end result isn't clear. Resilience is key to success. Anyone trying to accomplish a challenging goal will inevitably face many failures: some small and some so big that they tempt challengers to give up forever. It also helps to have support and encouragement. I have a loving and supportive wife who supports my dreams. She knew when I was hurting and offered regular support and encouragement. Surround yourself with people who lift you up when you're down and you'll find getting past your failures much easier.

After I hurt my knee, I could no longer run, but I had set a goal to break a Guinness World Records title. I hadn't given up on setting the 800-meter joggling record, nor did I even realize that it would be over a year and a half until I could run again, but I knew it was time to redirect my attention to a new goal for a season.

In 2004, I was a freshman at MIT pursuing a degree in Electrical Engineering. I took a physical education juggling class during the month-long January term which is called the Independent Activities Period (or IAP for short). It's meant for students to explore opportunities outside of the traditional semester. Students can take a concentrated for-credit class, get a 1-month internship, go overseas, stay at home, play video games, get some exercise, go on a service mission, or otherwise do whatever they think will benefit him or her most between the two all-consuming semesters.

I juggled.

I learned how to juggle when I was eight years old and had done a few juggling shows here and there throughout my childhood. I performed at events like the junior high school variety show, the National Junior Honor Society Induction Ceremony, and the Mr. Borah High School pageant (to this day, it's still the only beauty pageant I have ever entered or won).

I was a 3- and 4-ball juggler. Juggling 5 balls requires a much more serious application of effort. Learning to juggle 5 balls consistently takes dozens to hundreds of hours of practice.

When I took the PE class, I started juggling multiple hours per day. I went to the MIT Juggling Club (which happens to be the longest continually running drop-in juggling club in the world) that still meets on Sundays in the lobby of Building 10 on MIT's campus. I told some of the old-timers who could juggle 5, 6, or 7 balls that I wanted to learn to juggle 5 balls by the end of January, with a goal of 100 catches without a drop. They laughed at me and joked: "by the end of which January?"

Just a couple weeks later, after many dozens of hours of practice, I completed a run of 100 catches with 5 balls. Several long-time members of the club were thoroughly impressed and admitted their surprise. There were certainly "prodigy" kids who had mastered the craft quickly at a young age, but prodigy isn't usually discovered in college students. (To be clear, I'm not a prodigy.) A couple of them encouraged me to start a student juggling club at MIT to get access to funding, room reservations, and official status, but I'll get into that later.

In the 10 years between learning to juggle 5 balls and my present Guinness World Records title pursuit, I learned to juggle 6 and 7 balls and performed for audiences regularly with 5 balls. I was 10 years into 5 ball juggling when I found the record for "most juggling catches in 1 minute (5 balls)." I decided I would practice breaking that record while I waited for my knee to heal.

I started by measuring my baseline speed. I counted the number of catches I got in one minute while juggling 5 balls at my normal speed. I then counted the number of catches I could get in a brief time-period while juggling as fast as I could while sustaining a 5-ball pattern. I wasn't even close to record pace. Even when juggling so fast I could only keep the pattern alive for a few seconds, and I wasn't even close to record pace. I calculated my pace in catches per second, multiplied by 60 seconds, and found I had a long way to go. I decided to practice anyway. I practiced for about a week and then did another time-trial. I had barely improved. I was discouraged and decided maybe I wasn't cut out to be a speed juggler. I told myself that there's a physical limit to the speed at which humans can juggle. To think I could be faster than the best jugglers of the 7 billion people on Earth was setting my sights too high. Maybe there was a different juggling record I could attempt.

In the spring of 2015, I went on a Baltic Sea Disney cruise with my wife, her parents, and her brother. One of the entertainers on board was a professional juggler, Niels Duinker from the Netherlands. He was billed as a juggler with 4 Guinness World Records titles. I was still deep in my training for the Guinness World Records title for the 800-meter joggle, so

I visited with him after the show and asked him about his Guinness World Records titles. One was for the longest duration blindfolded juggling at 6 minutes, 29 seconds. When we got back to the room, I excitedly told my wife and brother-in-law, Kevin: "I could do that!" I had Kevin get out a phone to act as a stopwatch. Jennifer may have pulled out her cell phone to catch it on video. I closed my eyes and said "ready, set, go!" and I started juggling. I think I may have caught the first ball and then dropped the second on the ground. We all laughed at what a dismal failure the attempt was, and the moment was short-lived. I didn't try again that night.

A few months later, I decided I wasn't going to let a simple drop on the first time I'd tried something in a long time stop me. I was going to try again and practice with grit this time. There was no physical limit to blindfolded juggling - at least the limit certainly wasn't as cut and dried as speed juggling. To speed juggle faster, the balls must get as low, fast, and close together as possible without colliding. The physical limit can be calculated. To juggle blindfolded for a long time, you just need to consistently make an easy throw and catch a bunch of times. There is no obvious physical limit. I started practicing blindfolded juggling.

On my first try, this time I did much better than a single catch, and I rapidly improved. I was able to juggle for ten seconds, then twenty seconds, and then a full minute. I gained confidence. I realized that over the last 2 years I'd run over 2,000, miles and the vast majority of that was while juggling the basic 3-ball cascade: left-right-left-right over and over and over again for more than 250 hours. There were even times that I would be running down a wide street or an open track, and I'd let myself close my eyes while I ran and juggled. I'd catch the juggling balls on the back and downswing of my arm and let the tempo of my run dictated the timing of the next throw as my arm swung forward. My hand would release the ball, and as it flew up the unseen replacement would gently land in my hand as it swung down and back. I would let myself run and juggle with my eyes closed until I panicked, imagining I was about to run off the road or into a mailbox. I'd usually open my eyes to find I was still in the middle of the road.

When I wasn't running, my body had a lot less overall motion. Juggling with my eyes closed while standing in one place was sustainable for long periods of time. It also helped that the fear of running into a mailbox was removed. I had a consistent 3 ball juggling pattern from so much joggling. When I removed the running, I became even more consistent. I also told myself that I'd been practicing for 2 years already, so I should be good at this.

The positive feedback loop was strong. My blindfolded juggling improved, so I practiced with more confidence, which led to even more improvement. When I set a personal record (PR) crossing the 3-minute mark in a blindfolded practice run, I finally let myself believe "I am going to break this Guinness World Record!" I didn't just tell myself in gritty defiance; I believed it. I was elated, I was excited, and I was as determined as ever.

A few evenings later in my living room, I juggled blindfolded for 7 minutes. I broke the record. It was just a practice run, but I had proven to myself that I could break a Guinness World Records title. It wasn't official, and I still had a lot left to do to make it official, but I had proven to myself that I was capable. My childhood dream and newfound adult goal of setting a Guinness World Records title was within reach. Now I needed an event.

Guinness World Records has very detailed and strict guidelines on the requirements that must be met to officially set a record; they have a very high burden of proof. The upside is that if someone else breaks the record, I don't have to worry about being cheated by an unscrupulous character who makes a claim with insufficient or questionable evidence. If Guinness World Records says a record is broken, I know it's legitimate, and I don't have to wonder if I should still be the record holder.

The attempt is to take place in an area that is public or open to public inspection. There have to be multiple independent witnesses that have some standing in the community, aren't related to you, or the venue for the attempt, and have nothing to gain from the record being successfully broken. For time-based records, there needs to be multiple timekeepers using stopwatches accurate to 1/100ths of a second. Photo evidence capturing the record setup, start, attempt, conclusion, and wrap-up is required. The entire record attempt, including relevant setup, must be captured on video from start to finish with no breaks. (I always use a backup camera or two in case one goes out, gets knocked over or the vision is momentarily blocked which has saved me several times.) The attempt also needs to have an audience. Then all the details need to be filled out on several forms by the timers, witnesses, and the applicant. After that, all those materials are then submitted to Guinness World Records for verification. The nice thing is that this is all free if you're willing to wait. If you want to pay, they'll send an adjudicator on-site and the paperwork load is lighter.

I chose the annual Cradlepoint block party that celebrates our company's growth in a fun celebration on the Basque Block in downtown Boise. I asked the human resources department if I could use the venue and attempt to promote STEM education. They organized the event and said yes, so long as Marketing approved. I asked our VP of Marketing and he said he thought it would be a great idea if the executive team approved. I talked to the executive team and they said it sounded great if HR and the Marketing team approved. I figured I didn't need to go around the loop again. I had a date for my first Guinness World Records title attempt: October 2, 2015.

I kept practicing, and after warming up I could consistently juggle blindfolded over 6 and a half minutes every few tries. I even had a few runs over 10 minutes. What I didn't anticipate is how excited and nervous I would be for the actual attempt and how that would affect my juggling.

I had a phone interview with a local journal that had an intern write up an article about the record attempt.

The night before the attempt, I was so excited and nervous that I couldn't sleep. On the day of the attempt, I went to work like normal. In the afternoon, I hauled all my gear over to the block party site. It was windy. I talked to the band to let them know what was going to happen during one of their set breaks and started warming up. Then folks started showing up: witnesses, timekeepers, a giant clock used for road races for everyone to see, photographers, videographers, a local news crew, a local newspaper reporter, and finally the employees and guests for the block party. The record attempt garnered more attention than I had anticipated. I was introduced by a coworker, and I explained to the hundreds present why I was trying to set this record: to promote STEM (science, technology, engineering, and math) education. It was then time to don the blindfold and make my first official attempt to break a Guinness World Records title.

When I put on the blindfold, my sense of hearing and touch were amplified. I could hear the audience, I could feel my juggling balls, and I could both feel and hear my overactive heart beating much harder than normal.

I began juggling. Left-right-left-right-left-right. To maintain my focus, I count every sixth catch of the juggling balls in my head. I keep track of one ball: the last one I throw out of my right hand. I count every time it lands back in my right hand: one, two, three, four, five. When I count to five, I've made 30 total catches (10 of each ball and 5 of each ball in each hand). When I reach the count of 50 (300 total catches), I start back over at 1. Then I count to 50 again and so on. When I've counted to 50 five times, I know I'm just about at the 6-and-a-half-minute mark.

During the attempt, some folks shouted words of encouragement while others tried to shush those shouting. The wind gusted, but my juggling balls were heavy enough the wind didn't blow them out of my error tolerance. I heard all the noise but ignored it. I didn't care if they shouted or were silent. I was completely focused on the left-right-left-right and counting every sixth catch. Not unless someone had physically touched me or shouted right in my ear would an external factor have thrown me off. Except something did.

In practice, when I counted to between 250 and 262 (each count representing 6 catches), I was almost always over the 6-minute-29-second-mark. I often reached the record time of 6 minutes 29 seconds close to a count of 250 (1500 total catches). And yet when I counted to 262 in my head, the audience didn't react. I got more and more anxious. I counted up to 263, 264, 265. With each passing moment, I could feel the tension in my neck, back, and arms rising. I couldn't figure out why the crowd wasn't cheering. I was sure that if I had broken the record the audience would cheer. What was wrong? I kept juggling, left-right-left-right-left-right; one, two, three, four... thirteen, fourteen, fifteen. There were several hundred people in the audience, and I knew at least some of them would celebrate if I had passed the Guinness World Records title mark, but no one was making noise at this point. Sixteen, seventeen, eighteen, nineteen, twenty. I had never counted this high and not passed 6 minutes 29 seconds. What was happening? I soon found out.

I was so nervous and excited during the record attempt that I juggled lower and faster than I did in practice. This resulted in more juggling catches in the same amount of time. A lower pattern means the balls don't have as much variability in their landing point, but they're also more likely to collide with less space between then in the air. I also must make more catches without a mistake. With every passing second, my catch-count climbed higher than I thought should have been needed to break the record. My already high anxiety built to an explosion point. And then the audience erupted in celebration.

All the anxiety, excitement, and anticipation came rushing to the surface. It built for two years like a dormant volcano as I trained nearly every day to break a Guinness World Records title. The visible tremors and smoke came billowing out from the first throw of the record attempt. During the last few counts, while I waited for the audience to celebrate, the pressure became so great, I could no longer hold it back. When I heard the audience cheer, my nervous system erupted in celebration.

There was an instant and overwhelming adrenaline surge that shot through my body. My heart rate spiked, and I felt as if my heart would burst. I had so much adrenaline pulsing through my system I could have run away from a bear, but I could not juggle. I lost all fine motor control. The precision needed for blindfolded juggling was gone. I overthrew a ball with my right hand, it hit the outside of my left hand and fell to the stage just three seconds after the crowd had erupted in celebration. Fortunately, it was five seconds after I had broken the record since the big clock was started two seconds late. There was a collective sigh, a moment of disappointment, and then the celebration continued.

I was so thankful for all the people who had supported me on this multi-year journey and who helped me get through the failures and setbacks. I hugged my wife who was and is my biggest supporter. Without her support, this challenge would have been even that much harder.

I had finally broken my first Guinness World Records title. I had practiced with grit for two years. Having grit isn't just working hard, it's working hard for extended periods without giving up. It's pushing through the failures and setbacks. It's not making excuses. It's believing that you'll make it no matter what obstacles cross your path.

Longest Duration Blindfolded Juggling (3 balls)
Previous Record: 6 minutes 29 seconds
New Record: 6 minutes 34 seconds

3

HAVING A GROWTH MINDSET IS MORE THAN A FEEL-GOOD STRATEGY

Most Juggling Catches in 1 Minute (5 Balls)
Previous Record: 330 catches

In her book, *Mindset*, Stanford psychologist Carol Dweck describes two ways we can approach the skills and talents we acquire in life: with a fixed mindset or with a growth mindset. With a fixed mindset, skills and talents come from within and we're born with a fixed capacity for any skill or ability. We discover how good we are at something by trying it, taking a test, or being told. There is an upper limit to our abilities, and we shouldn't try things we're not good at since we want to avoid failure. People in a fixed mindset might say, "I'm not a math person," "I could never juggle," or "I don't remember names."

With a growth mindset, our talents and abilities can be learned and developed. People with a growth mindset enjoy challenges and pushing themselves. When they try and fail, they learn where their weaknesses are and can focus on improving in those areas. One of the most profound ideas I gleaned from Dweck's *Mindset* is that the belief that you can improve at something has a significant impact on your ability to improve at that thing. On one level, it seems almost self-explanatory, but on a much more profound level, it's astonishing.

One study that sticks out to me is where researchers had a group of people take a test and scored the results. They then randomly split that group into two. They primed one group with a fixed mindset. They said that this wasn't the kind of test one could study for. Once you've been judged, the results are consistent. And then they gave them study materials and time to study. The second group they primed with a growth mindset: they said this is the kind of test you can study for, and people can improve their scores dramatically if they study. They said you can get better at anything if you believe and work hard at it. They gave the second group the same study materials and the same amount of time to study. And then they had both groups retake the test. The results changed my view of the world. The group that was primed with a fixed mindset did not improve, but the group that was primed with a growth mindset improved and improved dramatically.

I tell students that when you're working hard on math or science homework that you need to believe you can improve. Be mindful of your internal dialogue because if you're saying things like "I can't do this," "It's too hard," or "I'll never be good at math." then you are sabotaging your efforts. Anyone believing that they can get better at something while working on it dramatically improves their chances of getting better at that thing. This applies to virtually any skill you want to learn in life.

I decided to take this new growth mindset back into my 5-ball speed juggling practice. I also now take it into all world record attempt practices and every personal and professional task that seems daunting at the outset.

When I first investigated setting this Guinness World Records title after I hurt my knee, I never really believed that I could be the fastest 5-ball juggler in the world. There are just too many people in the world and many thousands of jugglers much "better" at juggling than me.

When I set my first Guinness World Records title, I got a confidence boost. I realized I could be the best in the world at something, however insignificant. After I took Carol Dweck's growth mindset to heart, my 5-ball speed juggling practice started yielding surprising results. Instead of stagnating, with deliberate practice and a growth mindset, my trial runs showed marked improvement. Instead of telling myself "I'll try to maybe set this record," I told myself "I am going to set this record." With this attitude, it became much easier to put in the effort to make it happen. I went from getting only about 300 catches in one minute to 305. Then 310, 320, and finally 330 catches in one minute to tie the Guinness World

Records title during practice.

The juggling community maintains its own records database apart from Guinness World Records (with some cross-over) on JuggleWikia. Part of the hesitation that kept me from believing I could set this record was that the 5-ball speed juggling world record based on publicly available video evidence was 353 catches - 23 more than the official Guinness World Records title. If I had set up a video camera at home and caught that 330-catch run on camera, I would have had enough evidence to submit for the juggling record, but I was still 23 catches short. I didn't want to set a Guinness World Records title just to be denied the claim of the world's fastest 5-ball juggler since I hadn't bested the overall record. Guinness World Records has set the gold standard for veritability, but the person who set the overall 5-ball speed juggling record didn't meet those standards. Setting a Guinness World Records title for speed juggling is much harder than setting up a camera in a living room and trying to get one run on camera over several weeks. It's not just that the burden for evidence is so much greater, it's that the window to set the record is much smaller. You only have all the people and equipment necessary for evidence collection in place for a short time. Think of setting a Guinness World Records title as breaking an Olympic swimming record during an official Olympics heat. The other record would be comparable to setting it in a pool on a good day in any timed practice in preparation for the Olympics.

Even before I reached 330 catches in practice, I decided I was going to attempt to break both the overall and the Guinness World Records title 5-ball speed juggling records while adhering to the Guinness World Records rules. When I reached 330 catches, I didn't think for a moment that my work was done; it was just beginning.

Like the muscles I was developing with a fast-twitch response, the brain can be thought of as muscle with a growth mindset. It can be pushed, stretched, and challenged, and when it is, it grows - not in dimension, but capability. The challenge to juggle 5 balls fast is as much mental as it is physical. Virtually everyone can toss a ball from one hand to the other, especially when it's a low throw. The difficult part is having precise enough timing, force, and direction to make 6.5 throws and another 6.5 catches per second without a collision or dropping a ball. I had to tell myself I was going to break the record, practice with belief, and not give up.

In September of 2015, I introduced myself to Dr. Robert Kustra, the President of Boise State University, and shared that I had a goal of setting a Guinness World Records title at a STEM-related event on campus. He introduced me to Dr. Amy Moll, the Dean of Engineering, and she invited me to speak at the Science and Engineering Festival on campus in February of 2016. I kept practicing. On December 7, 2015, two months before the event, I was able to break the overall 5-ball speed juggling record in practice and was confident enough that I could break it live to let Boise State know I was going to attempt the record at the festival. With a growth mindset, my practice had yielded world-record worthy results. I had two more months to practice, and practice I did. I could break the record nearly every day if I gave myself a significant amount of warm-up time and had lots of attempts. I didn't want the audience to have to sit through an hour of me dropping balls with all the other cool activities going on at the festival, so I needed to become more consistent. What I should have been worried about was controlling my nerves. I practiced enough that I could regularly beat the higher 353 catch juggling record mark by over 30 catches! However, getting on stage in front of an audience of 500 people and trying to do the same thing was another matter entirely.

I organized a team of witnesses, timekeepers, videographers, and photographers. I also recruited a friend who would do some quick video editing, so we could play the video back in slow motion to get the official catch count during the live event since it's not possible for a human to accurately count 6.5 catches per second in real-time.

I put together a 30-minute juggling and balancing show to encourage students to pursue STEM education. I mixed in some of my life stories, highlighting many failures and a few successes. I wanted them to leave believing that if they set their minds to a goal and pursued it with a passion, they could accomplish anything. I was then going to set a Guinness World Records title to prove my point. On the week of the attempt, I realized that my show was more talking than juggling. It took me at least half an hour to warm up, so I'd have to do it before the show but during that 30-minute talk, my arms and body would cool down. My body needed to be fully warmed up and at its peak performance to do the fastest 5-ball juggling in the world. I decided to flip the script and attempt the world record first, so I could get fully warmed-up and attempt the record as soon as I got on stage. I would then have my friend edit the video and be ready to play it back in slow motion at the end of the hour to get the official count and validate the Guinness World Records title.

On the day of the attempt, my warmup was interrupted multiple times while briefing the three witnesses and three timers with all the requisite paperwork while explaining logistics as they arrived at different times. I also had to explain to the videographers the setup and verify camera positioning and the desired shots. It didn't help that one timer's car broke down on the freeway a little over a mile from the venue with his wife and kids inside. He ended up running the last mile while his wife and young kids waited for the tow truck. (Thank you, Jeremy and Beka!)

It was difficult to squeeze in enough warmup time. The upside was I didn't have free time to overthink the record attempt and get nervous with all the commotion. Only when I got on stage and told everyone I was going to attempt to break the Guinness World Records title that would make me the fastest 5-ball juggler in the world did I feel the adrenaline start working its way into my bloodstream.

Dr. Amy Moll introduced me to the crowd and I stood before the 500 people ready to prove the power of a growth mindset. I began my first attempt on a "ready, set, go!" and I dropped a ball almost immediately. "False Start!" I called out, and I tried again. I count every fifth catch during 5-ball juggling. I follow the last of the 5 balls thrown, and every time it lands in a hand, I count up one. I needed to count to 66 to tie the Guinness World Records title of 330 catches (that's the only one I told the audience about, even though I had a much higher personal goal of 353 catches which required making it to 71). On my first attempt, the pattern wasn't tight and fast enough and I worried I would land somewhere between 66 and 71 breaking one record and not the other. I didn't want to have to explain to the audience who would be celebrating a Guinness World Records title why I needed to attempt the record again to break the overall world record.

I got nervous and at about 30 seconds into the attempt, in a blessing in disguise, there was a ball collision. I may have been able to recover from it, but I decided to catch and collect all the balls instead. I stopped the attempt without dropping a ball. I got about 165 catches in 30 seconds (on pace for 330). After a pause, the audience decided to applaud and show their support and encouragement in a gesture I hadn't anticipated but appreciated.

On the next attempt "ready, set" was called and I threw a ball before "Go." I called out "Oops! I went too soon." The next attempt was better. I counted "1, 2, 3, 4..." up to "60, 61, 62, 63" for 315 catches. There were 7 seconds left on the clock and again, I got so nervous the pattern began to degrade. I had a mid-air collision and a ball dropped to the stage. The audience let out some screams and gasps and a collective "ooohhhhh!!!" since they knew I would have broken the record if I had finished the minute. The "ooohhhhh" from the audience started as a collecting groan with the low-pitched sound of disappointment and quickly turned into high-pitched screaming and cheering and clapping. They were excited that I was so close, then groaned that I didn't break the record. But then they got excited again with the hope that I would soon break it. They saw how close I was and wanted me to try again. The excited crowd began to talk to each other to let out the nervous tension they were feeling as well. On the next try, I made it up to the count of 60 before I dropped a ball again. This time the "ooohhhhhs" from the crowd were more painful and the pitch of the audience got lower as if they were experiencing pain. I took a long pause before the next attempt. I took a drink of water and did a little juggling run to calm my nerves. On the next attempt, I counted to 60 again and didn't drop a ball. I was nervous, but I kept juggling and the pattern stayed under control. I made it to 66, breaking the Guinness World Records title with nearly 7 seconds left on the clock. I kept going and counted up to 74 for 370 catches before the timer called time. Then the celebration began!

The presentation, talk, and juggling after the record attempt were anti-climactic. At the end of the hour, we reviewed the slow-motion video to get the final catch-count. As the team filled out paperwork, the kids began to line up to meet me. I saw them line up two hours earlier for Astronaut Steve Swanson. He was the other keynote of the day, and he posed for pictures and signed papers. Since I was at his presentation, I even jumped in on the end of the line and took a selfie of the two of us. I asked if he wanted to stick around to be a witness for the Guinness World Record attempt, and he politely declined. It hadn't dawned on me that kids would want more than to see me juggle and set a record. This was the first presentation I had done that kids lined up to get my autograph, take a picture, or both. I was happy to oblige realizing that perhaps I was inspiring these kids and perhaps encouraging some to work harder and believe they could be successful in their STEM subjects.

None of this would have happened if I didn't have a growth mindset. If I hadn't believed I could set this record, even with practice, I would not have improved. Nor would I have persevered without a growth mindset. It's not just a feel-good strategy; the research and science back up the claim that having a growth mindset affects results. And even though the strategy isn't just a "sounds good/feels good" strategy, the results sure felt good.

Most Juggling Catches in 1 Minute (5 Balls)
Previous Record: 330 catches
New Record: 370 catches

4

LEVERAGE YOUR STRENGTHS

Most Juggling Catches in 1 Minute (4 Balls)
Previous Record: 402 catches

After uploading the 5-ball speed juggling record to YouTube and posting a blog on my website DavidRush4STEM.com, I got a comment on my website from a Fr. Terry Donahue, CC. He wanted to inform me if I didn't already know, that not only did my 5-ball speed juggling record break the Guinness World Records title, but also the more informal records tracked by Juggle.Wikia.com (353 catches). He encouraged me to look through those records and attempt to break others. I had just spent months practicing for the 5-ball speed juggling record. Why not take that long-practiced skill and see if I could leverage the experience into a related record? It wasn't a Guinness World Records title (at the time they only recognized odd numbers of balls for speed juggling records) but why not at least try to break the 4-ball speed juggling record over a weekend? The record was 402 catches in one minute.

The most popular 4-ball juggling pattern is 4-ball asynchronous. That means 2 balls are juggled in each hand independently, and the throws from each hand don't happen at the same time. The throws are asynchronous alternating left-right-left-right with each ball making an inside to outside elongated oval motion landing in the same hand from which they're thrown. The balls in the right hand rotate clockwise while the balls in the left hand rotate counterclockwise. To juggle 4 balls as fast as possible, I needed to use a different pattern. Instead of the balls making a circular motion, each ball is thrown straight up, and the hands move back and forth to catch the vertically falling balls. There are still 2 balls being independently juggled in each hand asynchronously, but each ball has its own vertical column. The pattern is substantially different from juggling 5 balls. When juggling 5 balls, each hand does the same motion for every throw from the same location in a fluid, repetitive, circular motion. When juggling 4 balls, each hand is operating independently and performing a slightly different throw for each ball since the hand is in a different position for each throw (slightly to the left or right). While the pattern was different, I came into this one in a position of strength having just broken the 5-ball speed juggling record.

I decided to take up the challenge. I set up a camera in my living room to record one record-breaking run over the weekend while my wife was out of town. It was harder than I expected.

While there is significant leverage from the 5-ball speed practice, I hadn't been practicing 4-ball speed juggling and the effort didn't translate immediately. I was still trying to break a world record, which, for the record, is hard. I was leveraging my strengths but had an unrealistic expectation that I wouldn't have to work very hard. After several hours of juggling on Saturday, I gave up for the day. On Sunday, I tried again for a few more hours. I could juggle at record pace for 5 or 10 seconds and sometimes even 30 seconds, but as my arms fatigued, the throws got sloppier, and I struggled to finish a full minute at pace. I started to wonder if I was going to be able to break the record.

I decided I wasn't going to give up. Each time I dropped the ball or had a collision that forced me to stop, I picked the balls back up with even more determination. After several hours of trying with several breaks to let my arms recover, on Sunday afternoon, I juggled 4 balls for a full minute at what I thought was a record-breaking pace. I announced the result as 410 catches in 1 minute for the camera. It turns out I had miscounted. Fortunately, I was only off by 2 catches and 408 catches were still enough to break the previous record of 402 by 6. I posted the video to YouTube, and Juggle.Wikia was updated within hours.

I didn't spend months practicing for this record specifically, but in a way, I did. I had spent months practicing for another record and built a wealth of fast-twitch juggling muscle memory (or more accurately neuron memory). Once I had that strength, I was able to leverage it into another related pursuit. This same concept can be applied to virtually any skill you learn. There are always activities related to the ones you've practiced with varying degrees of leverage. There are adjacent tasks and challenges you may want or need to overcome, and it's helpful to leverage your strengths when you can. Sometimes you'll identify them yourself, and other times you may need to be challenged by a parent, teacher, or friend - or in my case - a friendly fellow juggler on the Internet.

Most Juggling Catches in 1 Minute (4 Balls)
Previous Record: 402 catches
New Record: 408 catches

5
PRACTICE WITH PURPOSE

Most Juggling Head Rolls in 1 Minute
Previous Record: 135 head rolls

Much has been written about the role of deliberate practice in honing a specific skill. To master an activity - be it soccer, an instrument, speaking, writing, dancing, or teaching - deliberate practice is required.

What is deliberate practice? It is a repetitive practice focused on improving a specific skill that includes immediate feedback. Deliberate practice isn't casually playing your favorite song or participating in a scrimmage game, it's focusing on the most challenging part of a new song or running a drill to work on a specific skill. The goal is to improve on that specific skill. If you master enough specific skills in a particular field, you can become a master in that field.

There are different levels of mastery, and you will pursue activities at different levels of mastery throughout your life. Some of us may never try to sing Opera; we won't have any mastery. Others will dedicate their lives to creating beautiful music. Some will play competitive sports and others will only play sport for exercise and entertainment. Some of you will be very good at managing your finances; the rest of us probably should be.

One measure of complete mastery, described by Malcolm Gladwell in his book, *Outliers*, is known as the 10,000-hour rule - sometimes called the 10-year rule. It is widely misunderstood. The common misconception is that it takes 10,000 hours to master a skill. This is misleading. If it took 10,000 hours to master a skill, none of us would master more than 2 or 3 skills in a lifetime besides eating and sleeping (and most of us still feel like we don't have one or both down yet). The 10,000-hour rule only applies to those who are at the absolute pinnacle of their profession. The very best in the world at chess, golfing, soccer, writing, speaking, music, and other widely pursued activities have usually practiced for at least 10,000 hours. Many other masters in each field haven't practiced nearly as long. A more realistic rule to master a skill is to apply about 100 hours of deliberate practice. With about 100 hours of deliberate practice, a person of average ability can master just about any skill. They wouldn't be the best in the world at it, but they could start from nothing and be ready to play a local concert hall, make the club soccer team, place in a local chess tournament, or be able to juggle 5 balls.

Some people participate in an activity their entire life and never really master it. Some people go fly fishing their entire lives, spend hundreds of hours doing it, and yet aren't masters. The reason is they aren't practicing deliberately. This isn't necessarily a bad thing. If the goal of the fly fisher is to enjoy the great outdoors, relax, and catch an occasional fish, deliberate practice may not be on the agenda. I would still challenge anyone to consider it. Deliberate practice is neither easy nor relaxing, but it can be very rewarding. Some people go fly fishing to relax and aren't concerned about their skill level. Others can't enjoy it unless they're doing their best and getting the fly to float ever so softly into the perfect patch of current to catch the largest fish. Those fly fishers should, and often do, spend time practicing deliberately.

The 10,000-hour rule isn't a hard and fast rule either. What it's trying to convey is that it takes a long time (many years) to reach the very pinnacle of a profession.

There is a learning curve for any activity. When we're just learning the raw skills of most new activities, we usually pick them up relatively quickly with deliberate practice. We go from having zero ability to just a little, to being able to do it. I've taught hundreds of people how to juggle in my life, and I see a clear pattern of skill acquisition. Some people have more natural talent, but just about anyone can learn to juggle. Juggling three balls is 95 percent mental. Virtually everybody can toss one ball up in the air to the other hand, catch it, and throw it back again. Juggling is doing that repeatedly with 3 balls each offset by ⅓ of the full cycle time (the time it takes for one ball to get back to its starting point). Some people pick juggling up more quickly, but almost everyone I've tried to teach how to juggle was able to pick it up within one to two hours of deliberate practice. Multiply that effort by approximately 100 and they could master 5-ball juggling. Multiply that by 100 again and they could be one of the best in the world (100 x 100 = 10,000 hours). I estimate I've spent about 5,000 hours of my life juggling, putting me at about halfway to 10,000 hours.

I may have spent more time playing soccer in my life than juggling, but most of the time I spent playing soccer wasn't deliberate practice. After high school, I primarily played games and scrimmages for fun. Yet I'm a much better juggler than a soccer player, even with more time spent on the soccer field. The difference is how the time on each activity was spent.

I played varsity soccer in high school, and we had regular deliberate practice. We would run drills focusing on a specific skill: passing, dribbling, trapping, heading, running defensive offsides traps, etc. We would run a drill once, get immediate feedback on what we did right and wrong, and then we would run it again. We'd repeat a skill over and over until we could execute it well on command. It wasn't as much fun as scrimmaging, but we got a lot better at what we practiced a lot faster.

When I played intramural soccer in college and recreational soccer as an adult, we would play games. We'd run around and compete, but not focus on any specific skill. I could get incrementally better, but much more slowly than when I practiced a specific skill. One of the reasons people shy away from deliberate practice is that it's not as much fun. You have to work on something that needs to improve meaning it's uncomfortable because you're at the edge of failure. Deliberate practice requires dedication, focus, and, most importantly, motivation. Without motivation, the best intentions to practice deliberately fall apart quickly.

One of the first juggling Guinness World Records titles I found and wanted to break was "Most juggling head rolls in one minute." A juggling head roll is done by placing the ball on the head with one hand and letting it roll off into the other hand while juggling instead of throwing it from one hand to the other. Instead of tossing the object up and over to the other hand, it's placed on the head and it rolls off into the other hand. The object gets to the same place but via the head instead of directly from the other hand. Each ball caught coming off the head is considered a single head roll. The record was 135 head rolls in one minute - over 2 per second.

When I first timed myself doing juggling head rolls, I was only able to do them continuously for about 5 seconds before I dropped a ball. I tried many times that day, and the results were all similar. I couldn't complete continuous head rolls with one hand for more than a few seconds unless I slowed way down. I was going to need to practice if I wanted to break this record.

The kind of practice that results in the most improvement in a learned skill is deliberate. I was already an expert juggler and could perform a head roll with little difficulty. What I couldn't yet do was quickly execute dozens of consecutive head rolls at world-record pace. I needed to get better by focused practice with immediate feedback.

I would begin a practice session by warming up my arms and body by juggling for several minutes. Then I focused on juggling head rolls. I would try the same skill multiple times. I would wear a stopwatch and count the number of head rolls I completed in a given time. I would calculate my juggling pace and track my improvement. I would track how many seconds I could sustain the juggling pattern before dropping. I would then try again and compare the results, making slight adjustments, and repeat the actions that resulted in better runs. I did this regularly for months until I could sustain a pace that substantially exceeded the current world record. My biggest problem was that while I could sustain a world record pace for upwards of 30 seconds, I couldn't consistently finish the minute. More practice was required.

I signed up to perform at the Idaho Kids Fair and told them I was going to attempt to break the Guinness World Records title for juggling head rolls. It forced me to buckle down and focus even harder, so I would be ready to finish the minute. My wife, Jennifer, knew I was practicing for this record, but says she doesn't remember ever seeing me complete a full minute run in practice because it was so difficult. I'm sure I did, but she may not have realized it was a full minute. She just saw me drop the balls time after time after time. The other reason she may not have seen a full minute run in the months of practice is that when I chose to buckle down the last couple weeks, much of my practice routine was at my office in downtown Boise. Every day at lunch I would go to the basement workout facility and put in a half-hour to an hour of deliberate practice on juggling head rolls. With those last two weeks of even more focused, deliberate practice, I was ready.

I got the Guinness World Records title verification team together at the Kids Fair. I was all warmed up, gave my talk, and then attempted to set this Guinness World Records title. On the first attempt, I got 141 juggling head roll catches before dropping one after only 42 seconds. The small audience wanted to cheer, but I let out a sigh of disappointment and told them that although I had just broken a Guinness World Records title of 135 juggling head rolls in one minute, I still had 18 seconds left and knew I could do much better. I had time left in the performance slot, so I made another attempt. It went perfectly. I completed 194 head rolls in 60 seconds. It was close to my personal record and beat the previous Guinness World Record mark by 59 catches, a 40% improvement.

If you want to dramatically improve any skill, you need deliberate practice. The skill could be athletic, like basketball free throws; academic, like solving calculus problems; professional, like giving presentations; or even social, like conversing with ease with people you don't know. If you don't practice, you won't get better, and if you do practice, practicing with purpose increases the rate of improvement dramatically.

Most Juggling Head Rolls in 1 Minute
Previous Record: 135 head rolls
New Record: 194 head rolls

6
FIND YOUR PURPOSE

Longest Duration Balancing a Chainsaw on a Chin
Previous Record: 1 minute 42 seconds

According to Angela Duckworth and her primary and secondary research, the people who stick with an activity long term consistently show two common traits: 1) the activity benefits them and 2) the activity benefits others. When people are doing something for purely selfish reasons they aren't nearly as likely to stick with it long term. If someone makes a ton of money, you might think that they'd stick with it so long as they can keep making a ton of money. Research shows otherwise. Once a person can no longer spend money in a way that increases personal happiness, the incentive to keep making more money goes away. This is often why people in careers that make a lot of money often leave those careers to focus on social and humanitarian ventures later in life (or more sadly look for fulfillment in addictive activities that often lead to losing everything).

In contrast, when someone does something that benefits someone else, but they don't enjoy it or don't receive anything meaningful from it, they're not likely to stick with it as long either. Burnout is common in social work and for youth pastors where it's all "give, give, give" if it's not balanced with proper appreciation and respect from the recipients of those gifts and the community. When an activity benefits both oneself and provides a benefit to others, people are much more likely to stick with it long term, i.e. rich business entrepreneurs who are also changing the world.

As I mentioned before, one of my first attempts at a world record was trying to mimic a man balancing a bunch of pint glasses on his chin. I used an empty cardboard carpet roll as I was pretty sure my mother wouldn't favor me using her glasses. It was about 12 feet tall, and I never balanced it longer than a few seconds. There are many reasons I didn't improve, but one of them is that I wasn't practicing for anyone but myself.

When I was a freshman in college, I took a PE juggling class, started the MIT Student Juggling Club, and spent a lot of time juggling. Balancing stuff on yourself and yourself on stuff goes hand-in-hand with juggling, so I decided to learn how to balance items on my chin. I started with a baseball bat and eventually got good enough to balance things on my chin for half a minute or more. I wanted to better myself, improve my performance repertoire, and entertain others. I had both motivation and purpose to practice balancing. It was a skill that helped me and entertained an audience. In my quest to find a Guinness World Records title to break, I also applied for the Guinness World Records title for the longest duration balancing a chainsaw on a chin.

This record was a beast. There are several reasons balancing a chainsaw on the chin is harder than a baseball bat or a juggling club. The first is that it's a chainsaw. The second has to do with physics. An object balanced vertically is an inverse pendulum with 2-axis of freedom to fall. A Segway is an inverse pendulum with 1 axis of freedom since it only tilts back and forth and not side to side. The Segway then senses the tilt and adjusts the center of balance to keep it from falling over. I had to do the same thing with an object on my chin but on 2 axes.

An inverse pendulum tips due to gravity pulling it down. Since it is fixed on the bottom, its tipping acceleration due to gravity is inversely proportional to the height of the center of gravity. This means the higher the center of gravity, the slower it tips and the more time I have to react to keep it balanced. A chainsaw has a big heavy engine right next to the handle that's placed on the chin, and a relatively light blade sticking up in the air. This means the center of gravity is low and thus it tips much faster than an object like a broom that has a skinny stalk and the heavy bristle ends up in the air. I like to say, in the most scientific way possible, that a chainsaw balanced on the chin is squirrely.

Much to the chagrin of my wife, I put in the time, energy, and effort to get strong and confident enough to balance a chainsaw on my chin. I signed up to give a talk and attempt to break this record at the Idaho

STEM Action Center FUNdraiser. Once I had a date, I practiced with even more fervor.

On the day of the event, I showed up to scope out the winery hosting the event to determine the best setup. I was going to attempt the record in the main room with the microphone and tables. I put the chainsaw on my chin to check out the backdrop when looking up at the ceiling. Practice in exact conditions is a very important detail when balancing an object on the chin. When I'm outside, the sun is usually the biggest problem since I can't stare into the sky with the sun in my field of view and keep my eyes open. I have found my eyes being open is still a critical part of being able to balance an object on my chin.

Inside a building, the problems can range from a bright light shining directly in the eye to a dark spot with no lighting on the object. There can also be moving objects like a fan, or, more troublesome, a slowly moving mobile or chandelier that throws off the stationary reference point needed to determine how much an object is tipping. There can also be objects hanging down that cause physical interference with the object on the chin. I didn't have any of those problems. I did face a different issue: the winery proprietor approached me. They said they were very nervous about the chainsaw falling and chipping their brand new and very expensive floor. I wasn't worried about dropping the chainsaw but could appreciate the concern. I said it wouldn't be ideal, but I could give the talk inside and attempt the record outside on their cement patio.

When the time came, I gave a 10-minute talk about the importance of STEM education with the supporters at the event and shared some stories from my wife's and my experiences. We both wanted to become engineers, went to MIT, and met there. After the talk, we all moved outside for the attempt.

There were a few problems. By this time, it was dark outside, so the lighting was limited to the stars which were not particularly helpful in illuminating the chainsaw. The lights inside shining through the windows were dim and lit only half the chainsaw. There was also a newly lit open fire pit blazing right next to the only place I could stand on level ground. I was also wearing a sports coat. If trying to balance the chainsaw on my chin wasn't hard enough, I now had to do it without being able to see it and knowing that if I had to make a move to the side to keep it balanced,

I might end up in the fire.

I had three witnesses signed up including Brad Little, the Lieutenant Governor of Idaho; Dave Hill, a Board Member of the State Board of Education; and 70 other people waiting on me, so I did what any insane person would do, I put on my leather gloves and went for the record anyway. I did ask several folks to turn their cell phone camera lights on and hoped for the best.

By my fourth Guinness World Records title attempt, I should have known better than to expect my body to remain calm and fully under my control. In practice, the chainsaw sat on my chin, and I slowly made minor adjustments to keep it peacefully balanced. It took strength, but after practicing, it was not difficult. During this attempt, I got nervous and I felt like a rubber stick flopping around since the extra adrenaline in my system had me shaking. I made it 30 seconds, then a minute, then a minute and a half. People whispered things like "I was here!" and cried out cheers of encouragement. My knees knocked together, but I was able to maintain the balance. When I passed the previous mark of 1 minute 42 seconds, I raised my arms in celebration, being careful not to accidentally touch the chainsaw in the process. When I hit two minutes, I put up three fingers signaling I was shooting for one more minute. I made it to three minutes and my neck wanted to be done. I pulled the chainsaw down.

I was elated. I was excited. I was enjoying myself and so were the 70 people in attendance. They were there to support STEM education, and so was I. I had a purpose. I had chosen to make my pursuit of Guinness World Record Titles about promoting STEM education. This pursuit would not only open opportunities for me to speak to students, educators, and the public about the importance of STEM but also gave me a message of encouragement. If you had asked me during this fourth Guinness World Records title attempt if I were going to break 20, I probably would have said it was unlikely. Over 150? Not a chance. But 5 years later, my pace had only picked up. I'm sticking with setting Guinness World Records titles for the long term because it helps me promote STEM education. I enjoy it, and so do others.

Longest Duration Balancing a Chainsaw on a Chin
Previous Record: 1 minute 42 seconds
New Record: 3 minutes 2 seconds

7
FIND YOUR MOTIVATION

Most Juggling Catches in 1 Minute With 3 Balls While Blindfolded
Previous Record: N/A (Guinness minimum set at 250 catches)

Without motivation, we do nothing. Hunger is the motivation that leads us to eat. Thirst is the motivation that leads us to drink. It's no surprise that hunger and thirst are so often used to describe people's goals and dreams. "We thirst for victory." "We're hungry for a win." The phrase "Be humble and hungry, or you will be" is one my CEO loves to use. The first part of the phrase is a metaphor: it means we need to be willing to receive feedback and admit we don't know or see everything (humility) and want more for our company (hungry). The last part is literal: if we don't have those characteristics, we will be humiliated (the company does poorly) and hungry (we will have no money for food since we'll be out of a job).

Motivation can come from either pursuing a reward or avoiding a punishment. They both work to motivate, but the far more powerful of the two is pursuing a reward - especially a non-material reward like happiness, fulfillment, or emotional satisfaction (known as intrinsic motivation). Material rewards (known as extrinsic) can also provide motivation, but usually only in the short term. We'll work a job for money, but if money is all it provides, the chances of losing interest are high. If, however, the money we earn at our job is used to provide food and shelter for our children, we'll continue working since the non-material reward of a child's health and safety is much more powerful than the money itself.

One of the most effective ways to stay focused on a goal and maintain pursuit is to visualize the prize. Visualize yourself winning, reaching your goal, and holding the prize. The more real you make the visualization, the better. Research shows that focusing on the end goal increases your chances of success. If you spend your time thinking about the obstacles, the pain, or the difficulties between you and the goal, you're much more likely to quit. Use the prize as motivation.

Another technique I use to stay focused on a goal is to abstain from something I enjoy until I reach my goal. This technique serves three purposes. The first is that it provides a little extra motivation for me to reach my goal. When I get there, I do not only get the prize from reaching the goal, but it also unlocks whatever I have been abstaining from. The second is that it may functionally help me reach my goal. For example, I may not eat any dessert until I set a world record for the fastest mile while balancing a pool cue on a finger. If I'm not eating dessert, I'm more likely to be eating healthy foods that help me run faster.

The third, and often most effective part of abstaining from something I want is that it's a reminder. Every time I want that thing, I remind myself that I'm on a mission. Every time I'm offered, think about, run across that thing, I have a reminder that I have a goal to complete. For example, my wife often goes to bed earlier than me, and I travel a lot for work and pleasure. I used to use those times to watch movies that I wanted to see that she didn't have any interest in watching. I am abstaining from watching any movie alone until I finish writing the first draft of this book. It frees up time to work on the book and serves as a built-in reminder to work on it. When I have free time, I naturally think about watching a movie which leads me to the keyboard instead. That reminder triggers an action to help me reach my goal. Focus on the prize and give yourself reminders that you have a goal. It's not quite the carrot and the stick. It's more the carrot with a smaller carrot dangling underneath and a small stick that keeps reminding me to look at and pursue the carrots.

Shortly after I decided to set the 800-meter joggling Guinness World Records title, I committed to abstaining from a few things that would direct my attention to reaching my goal. Focusing on the prize was the most important, but I increased my motivation (and, more importantly, resolve) by telling myself I would give up all soda, alcohol, and desserts until I broke a Guinness World Records title.

While this may not seem like much to some, for me it was huge. I work in the technology industry and alcohol is often served at events, trade shows, and dinners. Every time I declined a drink, I would think about my goals. I also drank soda regularly and decided to give it up. To make this one even more meaningful, I also didn't drink any naturally or artificially sweetened beverage, including juice. The desserts were the hardest and most meaningful thing for me to give up. I love candy and desserts. When I say I gave up dessert, I mean I didn't eat a single bite of a cookie, candy, cake, ice cream, milkshake, brownie, or chocolate. I didn't even eat a breath mint, cinnamon roll, or the M&M's from a bag of trail mix (I would eat around them.). I even abstained from chocolate milk and fruit smoothies.

I would make my wife milkshakes and when I scooped the ice cream, I would sometimes get a little on my fingers. Normally I would just lick it off, but for over a year I would wash my hands so as not to eat any dessert at all.

I estimated I cut out 15-25 desserts per week. Each one was a reminder that I was on a mission. The added benefit was that I was now eating 15-25 fewer unhealthy things per week that helped me get my body in shape for running. I lost about 25 pounds from eating less, running, and cutting out sweets, alcohol, and soda. I was trying to run a half-mile 15 seconds faster than I had ever run before, while juggling, and this technique helped immensely.

When I hurt my knee and was unable to run for over a year, my goal changed, but I maintained the incentives. I set the longest duration blindfolded record and then the fastest 5-ball juggling record. I also set the record for most juggling catches in 1 minute while blindfolded. It was the first Guinness World Records title I created. I think to this day I may still be the only one to have ever made an official Guinness World Record attempt for this title. Blindfolded juggling is hard enough but trying to do it fast gets frustrating if you don't first start with the fundamentals and get the individual components down first: blindfold juggling and speed juggling.

I decided to set this record at the FIRST Robotics Idaho Regional competition in Boise. It was the inaugural regional competition. FIRST stands for "For Inspiration and Recognition of Science and Technology" and has a key philosophy of "gracious professionalism." FIRST is a phenomenal program that gets youth of all ages involved in building robots in teams and competing. The growth and success of this program to both get students excited about STEM fields and to stick with it in their careers is outstanding. More than 75,000 high school students participated in 2016. They have programs for first to eighth-graders to get involved too. It continues to grow each year.

Since it was the first time Boise hosted a regional competition, there was a lot of excitement as well as organizational and logistical intensity compounded by the fact that Don Bossi, the organization president was planning to attend. The organization was excellent, and they brought in coordinators who had worked other regional events. I made a few contacts did some finagling to get myself on the schedule. I signed up to do a short juggling show and inspirational talk before attempting to break the blindfolded speed juggling record. I was elated.

On the day of the attempt, I showed up early to make sure everything was in order. Right off the bat, they tried to change the time of my performance. I explained that while I could be flexible, 10 other people were involved in making the world record attempt official. After a meeting with the organizing crew, they agreed to the original time slot but cut the amount of time from the 45 minutes I had prepared down to 20.

When we were sorting out the last-minute changes, the emcee had me follow him down the narrow tunnels of the stadium. I couldn't help but think of movies I'd watched with the protagonist being led down a narrow corridor and wanting to yell "Don't you see you're walking into a trap!" I knew it was just a funny thought until he pointed down a small hallway deep in the heart of a stadium that was an obvious dead end. The straight hallway had only an emergency exit a few dozen feet away. What I didn't see was that at the end of the short hallway, there was a small room off to the left. Six people were huddled around the operations command center. I finally figured out the emcee was just bringing me in to visit with the rest of the organizing crew.

I warmed up in the VIP lounge (mostly empty at that point) until just a few minutes before I was to speak. I then moved to the corner of the stadium to continue juggling, and so that I could see the action on the field without being a distraction.

I, however, was very distracted. I was so focused on the talk I was about to give, the record I was about to set, the schedule and program changes, and getting my team of witnesses and timekeepers to make it Guinness World Records official organized that I had little thought for anything else. I would have forgotten critical details like setting up and turning on the cameras required to gather evidence. Fortunately, my friend Becky was on top of it. It was one of the first record attempts she helped with and she took charge of setup, cameras, and other equipment, as well as teardown and clean up without any direction. It was only when I saw her wandering out of the arena an hour later alone did it don on me how much she'd done with so little direction or encouragement. I thanked her profusely and resolved to try to properly thank everyone who ever helped me out even when I'm busy and distracted. Without their help, my world-record-setting journey would not have been possible.

A couple of minutes before go time Becky set up the video cameras as I was introduced by the emcee. I took my spot in front of a thousand spectators and began my talk with how much I love a gathering of nerds. I decided to lead off with the MIT cheer and had this group help me out. "When I yell "I'm a beaver!" call back "You're a beaver!" and then I continued:

"We are beavers all.

And when we get together, we do the beaver call!

E to the u du dx,

E to the x, dx.

Cosine, secant, tangent, sine,

3 point 1 4 1 5 9.

Integral, radical, mu, dv

Slipstick, slide rule, MIT!

Go Tech!"

It was a fun way to start. I talked and juggled for about 10 minutes explaining how pursuing your goals with a passion can lead to great success. After finishing with how close self-driving cars are to becoming a reality and how we just sent a spacecraft to Pluto, I attempted to break the Guinness World Records title for most juggling catches in 1 minute blindfolded with 3 balls.

As this was a new Guinness World Records title, Guinness set a minimum mark of 250 catches in 1 minute to qualify. I did a dry run while blindfolded, explaining I would count every 3rd catch. To set the record I needed to count to 50 and then 34 (84 x 3 = 252 catches). On my first attempt, I made it to the count of 49 before I dropped a ball in only 21 seconds. I was on pace to not just break the blindfolded speed juggling record but also the overall speed juggling record of 422 catches in 1 minute. The crowd realized I had a good run and cheered even after a drop. On the second try, I counted to 48 before a drop. On the third try, I made it to the count of 50 and one.

Dropping a ball after only 20 seconds on all three times wasn't a coincidence. I started well each time, but when I made it to the count of 40, I got nervous and received a jolt of adrenaline. Just like when I set my first blindfolded juggled record, my fine motor control was negatively impacted by adrenaline. Blindfolded juggling is especially susceptible to nerves, and blindfolded speed juggling with extra adrenaline in the system is nearly impossible. More on that later.

On the fourth try, I made it a bit further, all the way to 50 and 27 with 25 seconds left. I was just a few catches away from breaking the record before I lost control and dropped a ball. I took a short break from juggling to explain that the hard things in life often don't come easily, and it's important to not give up.

On the fifth try, I finally broke the record. I made it to the count of 50, 50, and 1 before dropping (303 catches). I raised my hands in the air to signal that I had broken the record, but I wasn't satisfied. I had 18 seconds left on the clock. I was on pace for over 430 catches which would break the overall speed juggling record. I wanted to try again because I knew I could do better.

I checked with the emcee to see if I had time for one last try. I took a deep breath, tried to calm my nerves, and began the last juggling run of the day. I made it to the count of 50 with no issues. I then made it back to the count of 50 while fighting nerves. I held on for another count to 22 before dropping a ball again. It was my best run but still left me with another 10 unused seconds in the minute. I completed 363 catches in 50 seconds. I yelled "Good enough!" as I threw the balls to the ground and did a little more celebrating with the thousand people in the audience. I didn't break the overall speed juggling record, but I knew I could. I was breaking records to inspire others to accomplish their goals. I had found my inspiration and I supplemented it with external motivation. I broke this record, and while that was good enough for that day, I knew I'd come back to it again because I knew I could do a lot better.

Most Juggling Catches in 1 Minute with 3 Balls While Blindfolded
Previous Record: N/A (Guinness minimum set at 250 catches)
New Record: 363 catches

8
THE HABIT OF FORMING HABITS

Most Juggling Catches in 1 Minute (3 Balls)
Previous Record: 422 catches

If you had asked me if I could become the fastest juggler in the world before I believed in the power of a growth mindset, I'm not sure if I would have just laughed at you or given you a serious answer, which would have been "No!" But somewhere along the way, I started believing.

Breaking a record first requires belief. It requires a growth mindset. I have to believe I can get better at anything. It also requires grit. I have to practice – a lot. It requires a regular practice routine.

If you want to achieve a goal, it takes practice and perseverance. One problem is that life often gets in the way. Motivation can wax and wane, and we have so many priorities that we often fail to keep up with the important ones. When something is important, you should work toward it regularly. You need to set aside time and protect that time. You need to start doing it every day until it becomes a habit. Once it's a habit, it's a lot harder to break. It could be developing new skills for your job, setting aside time to date your spouse, training for a marathon, or breaking a Guinness World Records title.

Even with the best of intentions and a burst of passion to get started, it's hard to follow through on the bad days, the times with low motivation. Unless you've turned a behavior into a habit. I regularly develop routines to follow through on goals. I leave my keys and wallet on the island every day when I get home, so I don't have to go looking for them in the morning when I leave. I keep my biking clothes in the same place - visible in my closet - to make the habit of suiting up to bike to work in the morning a lot more likely to happen. For the first seven years of our marriage, my wife and I went to bed at the same time every night we were both in town, read a chapter out of the Bible, and said our prayers before going to sleep.

One routine that has been critical for me to break Guinness World Records titles is that I set aside my lunch hour to practice. Depending on the record attempt, I vary my practice routine, but barring a business conflict, I practice every day during lunch. My lunch hour varies in time and length based on meetings, but I make sure skipping it is the exception to the rule. For the first couple of years of Guinness World Records title training, I ran almost every day at lunch. Now it varies between juggling for a specific record, running to maintain base fitness, practicing a balancing activity, lifting weights - usually with an emphasis on the muscles needed for the upcoming record attempt - or practicing for a talk promoting STEM education.

I need this time as part of a daily routine to set the gold standard for speed juggling: the most juggling catches in 1 minute with 3 balls. I would practice nearly every day and sometimes for hours on the weekend. The deliberate practice needed to become a habit, or I would not have kept doing it. Trying to become the fastest juggler in the world isn't an easy task. I believed I could do it, but when I came back day after day and often didn't see any improvement, or even short-term regression, I would often only practice because it was part of my routine.

Outside of my routine, I would also practice whenever the chance presented itself. One of my most productive speed juggling practice sessions I had was on a plane headed to Taiwan from the United States for a work trip. I spent over two hours juggling in the back of the plane by the bulkhead, took a break for dinner and a movie, and came back and juggled for another two hours. It was the quickest flight to Taiwan I've ever taken.

I was hoping to break the 3-ball speed juggling world record during my blindfolded attempt, but nerves got the better of me, and I never juggled longer than 49 seconds in an official attempt (which was still enough to break the blindfolded record). I needed to find an event to showcase the fastest juggler in the world. The opportunity presented itself when my wife and I were on a date to our local movie theater at the Village in Meridian, Idaho. There was a sign soliciting entries into "Idaho's Got Talent." I was the first runner up the year before, so I was familiar with the event. To enter, I needed to create a short YouTube video. I put together a short show of juggling while I ate an apple. It was not my finest material, but I figured it would be enough to make it into the local competition. I uploaded the video and a couple of weeks later, I received word that I had been selected to compete. The semi-finals were Saturday morning, and the top five were given an encore performance slot to compete for the top prize.

I put together a 90-second show for the semi-finals with a short juggling and fast-talking routine ending with a ladder balance. I was fairly confident that it would land me in the top five, so I arranged to have witnesses, timekeepers, videographers, and photographers lined up for the finals. I had myself introduced as a multi-Guinness World Records title holder who was going to break the record for the fastest juggler in the world live on stage. My entire semifinal act built up to the Guinness World Records title attempt. But as I concluded my act for the semifinals (and as I had planned), I was out of time. All semifinal acts needed to be 90 seconds or less. It was now up to the judges to bring me back for the final and to see the attempt. During the feedback session, the local celebrity judges made a joke about putting them on the spot since the audience obviously wanted to see the record attempt.

My backup plan, in case something went wrong - i.e. I wasn't selected as a finalist - was to ask if I could attempt the record on stage after the end of the competition. Fortunately, I wasn't required to use my backup plan. I was announced as one of the five finalists and breathed a sigh of relief.

When it was my turn for the encore presentation, I got right to the point: I wasn't about to just become the fastest juggler in Idaho, not just the fastest juggler in America this year; I was about to become the fastest juggler in the world, ever.

I had practiced speed juggling so much during my routine lunch practices and for dozens of other hours that I was confident I could nail this record. I broke it a dozen times in practice in the hour leading up to the official attempt.

I brought the witnesses, timekeeper, and cameras to the stage with me and, after explaining all the evidence required to validate a Guinness World Records title, began my first attempt.

Ready, set, go! I started off juggling at a decent clip. After a few seconds, I got into the zone. The current record was 422 catches in one minute, and I was regularly getting over 450 catches and sometimes even more. My goal was 450 catches. About 30 seconds in, I started to get nervous. I was so excited that my arms started filling with adrenaline and my fine motor control degraded. The juggling pattern slowed. I tried to focus and speed back up but got more anxious. My throws were suddenly sloppy. I told myself I had to at least hold on and finish the minute. I was juggling painfully slowly for the last 10 seconds, but at least I was juggling. I waited until the timers yelled "time" and based on my audible count of 50, 50, and 45 (counting every third catch) I had achieved over 430 catches. The audience heard my count and as time expired and knew I had broken the record. I was so excited I let out a "Come on!" and the audience cheered. I didn't realize it right away, but my count was a little off.

As part of the celebration, I had one of the witnesses hand me a Guinness World Records certificate right there on stage for dramatic effect as if I were being officially awarded a Guinness World Record title. (It was the certificate from my first record, the longest duration juggling blindfolded.)

We gathered up the cameras and loaded the video onto my laptop so we could later confirm the official count. In the meantime, they brought the five finalists back on stage and announced the winners. I placed a disappointing fourth of the five finalists. I realized that setting a speed juggling Guinness World Records title live is much harder and a lot less entertaining than a simple juggling comedy routine. If I had wanted to win, I should have done a juggling routine that looked and sounded more fun but was a lot easier to pull off. The contest was also put on by a radio station, and I suspect that the musicians were going to be favored by the judges with musical backgrounds unless there was a novel act that blew them away. Mine did not. They did all give positive feedback and said that if anything inspired kids to pursue STEM, it would be my juggling.

We took the computer into a nearby restaurant to get out of the sun so we could see the screen and counted the catches in slow motion. It was only then I realized my original count was not accurate. I have attempted many records since and have noticed a pattern in the timing process. There is almost always a slight time delay from the end of the minute until the audible "time!" reaches my ears so I keep counting a little too long.

When we counted to 428, the playback stopped unexpectedly. I had clipped the video at exactly a minute and wondered why it had stopped prematurely. Only then did I realize how narrowly I had broken the record – by only 6 catches. I would have felt bad had I misled the entire audience. Fortunately, the result stood and nearly 16 months later was published in the 2018 print edition of Guinness World Records.

Breaking the 3-ball speed juggling record was one of my proudest achievements. I could now claim to be the world's fastest juggler. A claim that even a few months before seemed nearly unfathomable. Make no mistake, I do not think this makes me the "best" juggler in the world. Speed juggling is not a skill practiced by most professional jugglers as it doesn't make for great stage entertainment. But it is still an important record for me. Right before I began the attempt, I introduced my son and said that while he had been to every one of my world record attempts, this would be the first one he would be considered present for since he was only a few weeks old. As I dedicated the attempt to him saying "This one's for you," I choked up and nearly started crying.

This record was made possible because I practiced regularly. I had a routine. I reserved my lunch hour at work. If you want to start a routine, you can pick whatever time works for you. For many people, the first thing in the morning is the best time. Putting something off often means it doesn't get done at all. You may have kids or a significant other who will demand your time later, and it's hard to say no. Whatever time you pick, protect that time until it becomes a habit. Don't expend extra energy trying to decide what you're going to do today when you've already set your goals. That's the beauty of habits and routines. There is scientific evidence that spending energy making a choice or a decision on one thing leaves less mental energy for other decisions. This is why Facebook founder Mark Zuckerberg claims he wears the same clothes every day: so he doesn't have to decide what to wear and can save his mental energy for other decisions.

Once you have a habit or a routine set, you can spend your mental energy making yourself a better you instead of spending that energy convincing yourself to spend time making yourself a better you.

Most Juggling Catches in 1 Minute (3 Balls)
Previous Record: 422 catches
New Record: 428 catches

9
PAY ATTENTION TO DETAIL

Most Selfies in 3 Minutes
Previous Record: 118 selfies

Details matter. Sometimes. When the details matter, spend time on them; when they don't, don't. I like to joke that Guinness World Records is the "Guinness Book of Prove You Did It." To guide potential Guinness World Records title challengers, a 25 page 'Guide to Evidence' details how and what to document for each world record attempt. In addition to the guide, there are specific rules that must be followed exactly for each record. Some rules apply for all time-based records and others that apply for all distance-based records. I've found that strictly adhering to these rules is mandatory for both timely processing and eventual validation of a record attempt.

I'm always on the lookout for potential Guinness World Records titles I could break, so when I saw a news article on Dwayne 'The Rock' Johnson and his successful attempt to break the Guinness World Records title for most selfies with different people in 3 minutes, I was intrigued. I suspected that since he's been one of the highest-paid movie stars for several years, he probably didn't spend all that much time practicing for this Guinness World Records title. I figured that with some effort and access to some motivated people, I should be able to surpass the mark. It was my first foray into mass-participation records.

The first step was to submit my application. Several weeks later the application was approved.

Only after an application is approved can you make an official attempt to break a record. In fact, only after an application has been approved do you even receive the record-specific guidelines. Sometimes the record sounds easier than it is until I get the rules. For example, I once saw the record for most balloons burst simultaneously with a bow and arrow. The record was seven and I was sure I could line seven balloons up in a row to break them all with a single shot from an arrow. Only after receiving the rules did I discover that all seven balloons had to be burst with seven different arrows shot off the bow at the same time. Instead of risking the lives of whoever may have been downrange, I canceled the application.

The selfies record included rules such as 1) "For the purpose of this record a selfie is defined as a photograph that one has taken of oneself." 2) "Selfies will include the full photographer's face and at least one additional person's face in full." 3) "All selfies must include at least the full face of the photographer and the full face of at least one other person. Both faces must be fully included in the selfie." 4) "All selfies must be in focus and sufficiently bright to enable the participant appearing in the picture to be recognized and identified as a unique participant to the record attempt." 5) "All selfies must feature all or part of the arm used to hold the phone or tablet." 6) "The same person cannot appear with the participant in more than one selfie." 7) "The participant may choose to photograph more than one person in the selfie, but all people photographed cannot be photographed again." 8) "No accessories including selfie sticks can be used to take the photos."

And that's only half of the rules specific to this record.

One rule that was unclear to me was if a digital camera could be used or if it had to be a cell phone or tablet. I contacted Guinness World Records for clarification since I figured a high-end DSLR digital camera could take pictures in focus while moving in possibly poor lighting conditions a lot better than a cell phone. The contact at Guinness World Records said a digital camera was fine so long as it was handheld.

The other big improvement I thought could be made was how to rapidly photograph and process as many different people as possible. I thought through several different possibilities. One that still intrigues me, but I couldn't figure out how to pull off, was arranging a long line of people shoulder to shoulder facing to the side. I would then run down the line while snapping continuous pictures. In that scenario, the people would have to be sufficiently far apart so as not to appear in the other photos, and I would have to remove all the pictures where my face was blocking theirs. If I were taking continuous photos it might be possible, but that would essentially be a video and not adhere to the spirit of the rules for this attempt.

Another idea that I still think might work well is to have a large group of people all in the frame but covering their faces and necks with a poster held up in front of them and then have them sequentially reveal their faces for their selfie and cover their faces during everyone else's selfie. I eventually scrapped this idea due to the logistics and practice necessary to pull it off. I suspect if properly executed, that method would make it possible to take more than 250 selfies in three minutes.

The plan I eventually chose was to form two lines of people to enable parallel processing. I would have one line on either side of me, and as I took a picture on one side, the person on the other side would get into position. I would then move back and forth left-right-left-right (mostly by leaning) and take pictures with people on alternating sides.

While it sounds easy enough to explain, several nuances make it more difficult than it sounds. One overlooked detail would ultimately disqualify my official attempt.

The rules clearly state that I'm the only person allowed to appear in multiple selfies. I could take a selfie with a group of people, but none of them would be allowed to appear in any additional selfies. Since I planned to have people on either side of me, a focus of my practice was to point the camera to capture me and one other person without moving it too far in either direction. Too far toward the side, and I risked cutting myself off and/or adding the next person in line. Not far enough to that side, and I risked cutting off the person who I was trying to capture with me. Or I could capture the person on the other side that I had just shot or was about to shoot. I then had to make this transition from left to right successfully at least once every 1.5 seconds.

I practiced by taping multiple balloons on a wall just behind me to represent peoples' heads. I put up a balloon on each side representing where people would stand for the selfies and another balloon on each side a little further out representing the next person in line on each side. I had to fully capture myself and the first balloon, but none of the next balloon. I quickly discovered how hard it was to accurately point the camera at the right spot 100 times in a row. The disadvantage of not using a smartphone is that I didn't have a live shot view to help me frame the picture.

Sometimes I would fail to capture my forehead, other times I would cut off my chin, and often my neck or arm was missing. Sometimes the balloon would be only partially in frame. The biggest problem was that I would too often capture the second balloon on the same side representing the next person in line. The second balloon was in frame nearly every time until I made two big adjustments. The first big adjustment was to physically move the camera body side to side instead of simply turning the camera to point it left and right. When I turned the camera without moving the body, I would point it so far left or right that it would capture the next person in line. Instead, I learned to keep the camera facing straight back at me as I moved myself and the whole camera from side to side. I had to swivel the lens a little so the extra space in the frame for another person was to my left or right, but nowhere near as much as when the camera body didn't move laterally.

The second big change I needed to make was how I had people form the two lines. They obviously couldn't be coming from behind me on the left or right or they would be in the preceding selfie. But even lining people up on either side of me along a wall that I was backed against required near-perfect camera framing to avoid capturing the next person in line. The change I needed to make was to have them come into selfie position at an angle both in front of and to the side of me. The two lines of people would make a "V" coming in for the selfies. It required the person to turn more than 90 degrees to face the camera which may have slowed the process, but at least the selfies would count. To prevent people from lining up along the wall, I considered having something set up against the wall like a trash can, so the line would be forced to move away from the wall as it approached me. I also considered what it might look like to have a trash can in every selfie I took.

Another big piece of the challenge was being able to hold a full-size digital camera at arm's length while moving and pointing it left and right reliably without my arms either getting so tired that I wouldn't be able to hold the camera up, or shaking so uncontrollably that the pictures would blur. I practiced with the camera, lifted dumbbells in the weight room, and eventually found a lighter camera.

The next step was to find an event where I'd have access to over 105 people, preferably closer to 150 so I could go faster and have some buffer in case a few pictures were disqualified. Following the theme of promoting STEM education, I picked the Idaho Day of Design put on by the local library system and Idaho STEM Action Center on July 25, 2016.

The weekend before, I was at my church's family camp at Ponderosa State Park in beautiful McCall, Idaho. One of the nights we gathered for skits and games. I decided to make one of the games an audience participation Guinness World Records title dry run. I got all one hundred folks there to do a full dry run of the selfies record. It was a high energy event with so much excitement it was almost as if we were trying to break the official Guinness World Records title. The practice went well, but I learned a very valuable lesson that helped me immensely when I attempted the record. Many of the participants were young children much shorter than me. When a child is standing next to me, they tend to stand back and hide behind me, so my arm blocked many of their faces. I never had this problem with the balloons since they were always in the same spot where I put them – just a little lower than my head. I made an adjustment to hold my arm lower when there was a shorter person next to me to ensure their entire face would be visible. This proved a critical adjustment for the official attempt.

On the day of the attempt, seminars in the morning led by TinkerCAD taught their classes how to use the Maker software to design 3D models. I counted about 175 people at the event. A detail I discovered less than a week before the attempt was that the record had been broken again and it now stood at 118 selfies instead of 105. I would need to ensure that most of the participants stuck around if I were to have enough to make the official attempt. The class participants were supposed to get out of their classes at 11:45 AM, so we scheduled the record attempt at noon. At the end of each session, each presenter agreed to give instructions to head out to the main exhibit room to attempt to break a Guinness World Records title.

I was setting up the lighting and video cameras and briefing the witnesses when I noticed one of the classes was filtering out at just after 11 AM. I raced over and asked the participants if they were planning to say for the Guinness World Records title attempt. They looked at me with puzzled expressions. I realized the instructor hadn't announced the record attempt. Worse still, they had been asked to leave, get lunch offsite, and come back at 1 PM. I tried to catch several people and tell them about the world record attempt and ask them to stick around until noon, but I couldn't reach most of them. Those I did reach already had it in their mind they needed to leave to get lunch. Since it was also the largest class with over 70 people, if I lost most of them, I wouldn't even have enough people to attempt the record, let alone have any margin for error.

I held out hope and tried to convince everyone at the conference center I saw to come into the room at noon. I brought my sound system and microphone in case there wasn't one on-site, and I'm glad I did. At noon, I used my sound system to explain who I was and that we were going to attempt to break a Guinness World Records title. I had all the people line up in two lines and a couple of volunteers helped me count them. The count revealed that we only had one hundred people. We needed 118 to even start the attempt.

I didn't want to give up just yet. I asked a dozen people to go scouting for any people in the conference building. There were a few stragglers in the classrooms, there were a few in the foyer, and there were the facilities organizers that joined. I also had Ken Hosac, my coworker, convince the coffee baristas in the lobby to come join as well. We eventually had 122 people in line. That was just enough to make the attempt, but I had to make every selfie count.

I got them excited and ready to go by filming the two lines of people with my handheld video camera as I ran up and down each line. I then got into position for the first selfie and began after a "ready, set, go!"

I began taking pictures, alternating sides for each shot left-right-left-right. I could take over 60 selfies a minute in this arrangement, but I only had two thirds the number of people required to go that fast. I chose to go slower and be deliberate to make sure every selfie counted. I framed each shot, made sure my arm was not blocking any faces, and confirmed that the shutter clicked for every person. I was still going fast, but only about 70% of my top speed. With ten seconds to go, we were running out of people. One line emptied, so I was only taking selfies on one side. Then there were no people left. That's when the news cameraman came and took the last selfie with me with the large video camera still on his shoulder. I took the selfie with him just before time expired.

I wasn't yet sure if I'd broken the record. I loaded the pictures onto a computer and when I started paging through them, I immediately noticed a problem. The two official timers that were timing the event were standing behind me on one side. Their faces were small as they were several steps behind me, but they were recognizable in about a third of the pictures. (It wasn't half since they were sometimes blocked by the person next to me.) According to the rules, the pictures could be disqualified, but we decided to make a judgment call and hoped the timers in the photos wouldn't disqualify the attempt. By the time we figured this out, some people had dispersed so it wasn't feasible to repeat the attempt.

We counted all the unique selfies and announced to the crowd - we had achieved 128 selfies for a new Guinness World Records title.

Or so we thought. I submitted all the evidence to Guinness World Records and a few months later they wrote back that my application had been unsuccessful. They counted up all the pictures the timers behind me showed up in and subtracted all but the first from the 128-selfie total. That total was less than 118, so my attempt was deemed unsuccessful.

I had done so much work and paid attention to so many details. I had worked hard and just barely gotten enough people. I practiced many times with balloons. I even did a dry run practice with 100 volunteers. I read the rules several times. But in the end, my entire effort was derailed by the smallest of details.

Sometimes it's worth worrying about the details; sometimes it's not. Was the laundry folded perfectly? Did the company-internal PowerPoint presentation have the very best graphics? I try not to worry about those details. But sometimes, the details do matter.

A few weeks later, I got a letter from the Mayor of Boise congratulating me on breaking yet another Guinness World Records title promoting STEM. I was proud to have received it and was happy to be promoting STEM education, but some wind was taken out of my sails when I found out the record was disqualified. I updated my website and the YouTube video and did another post on social media noting the attempt had been disqualified. It wasn't a pleasant experience, but I certainly learned from it. I would go on to attempt this record again at my MIT 10-year reunion with notably better results. But first I had to learn from this setback.

My main consolation was that my goal of promoting STEM education was still achieved. Kids were excited to be part of a world record attempt and they were excited about learning 3D modeling software. I was still able to talk about the importance of having a growth mindset when trying to improve at any skill or ability. I had a failure and a setback, but it was not a permanent condition. I would go on to break this record later while paying just a little more attention to the important details.

Most Selfies in 3 Minutes
Previous Record: 122 selfies
My Attempt: 128 selfies minus about 50, for an unsuccessful result

10
DON'T FEAR FAILURE

Most Juggling Catches in 1 Minute Blindfolded (3 Balls)
Previous Record: 363 catches (held by me)

My first year of breaking Guinness World Records titles exceeded my greatest expectations. I may have failed to set the record I had trained for the most: the fastest 800-meter joggling, but I pivoted to others that allowed me to build confidence. Twelve months after breaking my first Guinness World Records title, I had broken more than a half a dozen. Little did I know the icing on the first-year record-breaking cake was yet to come.

Most of the communication I have with Guinness World Records is through email and their web portal. The emails are mostly automated messages triggered by application submissions, application approvals, and record approvals. I received automated emails from Guinness World Records so often that I didn't think much of the one congratulating me on making the 2017 Guinness World Records book and asking if I'd be interested in coming to New York City for the book launch. It included an offer for me to attempt to break one of my existing records or a different one during the book launch week.

I was stoked to know I was going to make the print edition of the book as less than 10% of all the records make it to print each year, but I wasn't sure if there was a catch. I assumed this email went to every person who made the book, and I had no idea the selection criteria or cost to participate. I replied that I would love to hear more details, figuring I probably wouldn't get a response, or if I did, it would come with an exorbitant cost to participate.

A few days later, a Guinness World Records representative reached out asking which records I'd be interested in breaking and suggested a follow-up call. It was on that call that I discovered only a handful of individuals were asked to participate. The representative was going to start lining up media agencies to see if any were interested in any of the records I offered. I quickly put together a list of records that I would be willing to break again, as well as a few others I had been practicing and thought I could get ready to break in time.

I let myself believe for the first time that I might actually go to New York City to break a Guinness World Records title. As a child, I read through the books and watched the Guinness World Records specials on television imaging what it would be like to be the one making the record attempts. I had broken several Guinness World Records titles which had fulfilled a lifelong dream, but none had more than local news coverage. I had worked so hard and now I was within striking distance of another dream: breaking a Guinness World Records title for a national audience.

I tempered my expectations by remembering that several people had received invitations. I might not be chosen.

I don't know what the actual chances of being selected were, but after a couple of follow-up emails, Guinness World Records confirmed that they had scheduled me on the TODAY show to break the Guinness World Records title for most juggling catches in 1 minute with 3 balls while blindfolded, also known as the world's fastest blindfolded juggling.

I was in shock.

I was excited. I was nervous. I had less than a month to prepare.

The first order of business was to look up and figure out what the TODAY show was. I don't watch much TV, and never in the morning, so I didn't know much beyond it being a morning talk show. I found out it was watched by about 5 million people per day and it runs for 4 hours every morning. The biggest surprise for me was that it airs live. It turns out I would have been better off not knowing that detail.

I felt confident since I already held the record. I broke it at the FIRST Robotics Idaho Regional competition in Boise that April. They had to expedite the review of the record since it was still pending in the Guinness World Records system. The official mark I set and had to beat was 363 catches in one minute. What that number didn't capture is that I set the record in only 49 seconds of blindfolded juggling. After 49 seconds, I dropped a ball. Since I had broken the record and was running low on time, I didn't attempt it again.

All I had to do on the TODAY show was finish the minute to break the record. But I set my sights higher.

In April of 2016, I broke the Guinness World Records title for fastest juggling with a run of 428 catches in a minute. When practicing, I would often have runs of over 450 catches in a minute. When practicing blindfolded I was slower, but not by much. My juggling pace for blindfolded speed juggling of 363 catches in 49 seconds is over 7.4 catches a second. Multiply 7.4 catches per second by 60 seconds and I was on pace for 444 catches. If I kept up my blindfolded speed juggling pace for the full minute, I could break the overall speed juggling record... while blindfolded.

When pursuing a goal, research shows that visualizing the prize, imagining achieving the goal, and experiencing the emotions that come with success help people maintain motivation. Visualization helps people continue working hard toward their goals. This by no means replaces the need to pursue the goal, but instead enhances the anticipation and provides incentives. If instead, a person focuses on the fear of failure and imagines the agony of defeat, they are much more likely to lose motivation. At best, they practice out of fear instead of practicing with purpose.

I visualized my goal of breaking the overall speed juggling record while blindfolded. I imagined the emotions. I got giddy. I could see the headlines. I wasn't just attempting to become the fastest blindfolded juggler in the world. I was going to become the fastest juggler in the world. Period. While blindfolded. The thought was so insane, so implausible, so shocking - even to me - how could it, with 5 million viewers, not be the crowning achievement of my juggling life?

And so, I practiced more.

I practiced every day, usually multiple times per day. I got good enough that with only a short warm-up I could usually break the record. In a typical practice session, I would break the record dozens of times.

I kept pushing myself to get faster and faster. If I got fast enough, I could back off from my physical limits during the actual attempt to have a comfortable run and still break both records. If I were forced to be my absolute best on live TV, I worried the pressure might be too much.

My wife, 4-month-old son, and I went on vacation to the Grand Canyon in the weeks leading up to the attempt. I took my juggling balls with me. When we put Jeremy down for his twice-a-day naps and early bedtime, I would get warmed up and practice blindfolded speed juggling. Run after run after run of 3-ball speed juggling. I would start my stopwatch and count every third catch. I would get immediate feedback from the result and adjust accordingly. I was getting faster. I made a run of almost 470 catches in 1 minute with my eyes closed, smashing both records.

I told my family, friends, and coworkers about the TODAY show appearance, and they got excited for me. I only mentioned that I was going to attempt to break the blindfolded speed juggling record and left off my real goal. I wanted to surprise all my family and friends and make them proud.

Guinness World Records booked my flight and hotel. My wife, Jennifer, loves to travel so she decided she would come as well with our son, Jeremy She also loves tennis and convinced me we should stay the weekend and see the US Open Women's tennis final with friends while there.

My biggest concern leading up to the events was my nerves. When I originally set the record at the FIRST Robotics Idaho Regional, it took me several attempts. The main reason I dropped the balls wasn't that I was blindfolded; it was because I got nervous and my arms turned to jelly.

I decided I would be super prepared to the point where I could be far from my best and still set both the records. As a fallback, I could be terrible and still set the blindfolded speed juggling record which would have maintained the appearance of success to everyone watching. Knowing this, I told myself the pressure was off. I still wasn't sure how I was going to handle the moment and had no way to accurately simulate the pressure.

The Friday morning of the attempt, the hotel staff let me into the hotel ballroom, and I went through my 45-minute-long warm-up routine. The limo sent by the TODAY show was a few minutes late picking us up from the hotel, so we arrived at the studio a few minutes after we were scheduled, but we still had plenty of time. As we pulled up to the studio,

Neil deGrasse Tyson, the famous astrophysicist who brought science in movies to the masses, was just leaving and getting into the limo in front of us. If I had been prepared for the moment, I would have jumped out of the car to introduce myself as going on the show to promote STEM education (which is a lot of what he does). Instead, I simply exclaimed to my wife that there was Neil deGrasse Tyson and whipped out my cell phone to take a picture. He gave a sideways look as he got into his car and didn't appear to be too thrilled.

Upon heading in, I was grabbed by the somewhat frantic show producer who explained I was late, and we needed to go quickly. I didn't think the car was that late. As I followed her hurried footsteps, I said we needed to slow down so my wife and child who were just a few steps behind could keep up. She gave me a shocked look and said we couldn't just bring anyone in. At that point, we were forced to dive into a side room as the show hosts were making their on-air morning walk outside during the live broadcast. In the small closet, I explained that Jennifer and Jeremy were expected and prearranged. She said her assistant must not have informed her. I didn't think I had been working with an assistant. It was at that moment she decided to ask me who I was for the first time. I said my name was David Rush and she said, "You're not my guest, are you?" I said I was there to attempt a Guinness World Records title, and she confirmed that I wasn't her guest indeed. The hosts had walked outside, so I was free to go back through the hallway and to the lobby to reunite with Jennifer and Jeremy.

The three of us headed downstairs and met up with the correct host. I met the Guinness World Records adjudicator and watched as he took the certificate with my name on it and mounted it in the frame for presentation after the successful attempt. I kept practicing in the green room to stay warm and broke the record time after time. I was completely calm. I kept wondering if and when I would get nervous, but so far all I felt was a little excitement that didn't affect my ability to juggle.

As we waited in the small room, Hoda Kotb walked through and was immediately drawn to my 4-month-old son, Jeremy. I was holding him while taking a break. Hoda was the 10 AM show host I would join on set in just a few minutes. She was cooing at him and poking his belly. It was a special moment. I introduced myself to Hoda, and only when she looked at me with a quizzical look did I realize that she had no idea who I was. She interacts with many guests every day, and I suspect there are many guests she never meets before their time on set, and many she never sees again. The only reason she was seeing me was because I was holding a 4-month-old baby. Six months later she was on maternity leave welcoming her first child (adopted) at the age of 52. I think I know why she was so baby conscious.

Just before going to the next and final green room, I was taken to makeup to get a very quick coat of powder to prevent glare, and then we were shuffled to a small room. I did a couple of quick practices with the Guinness World Records adjudicator to practice the start, and then we went on set.

It was still a few minutes before the live broadcast, so I took my place in front of the 3 giant cameras and blindfolded myself for a couple of practice runs to see if being on set made me nervous. I didn't have any trouble.

Then the hosts Hoda Kotb and someone I'd never heard of before, Billy Bush, came on, and they played a pre-made segment introducing me as "the blindfold juggler." It called out several records I currently held and scrolled through several pictures of me juggling in front of landmarks from around the world.

I had prepared a few minutes' worth of talking points about how I was breaking records to promote STEM education and how it tied to Carol Dweck's growth mindset. I had even emailed Dr. Carol Dweck hoping to get a little personal insight, using the TODAY show appearance as my hook. Regrettably (but understandably), Dr. Dweck never responded.

When we were on set, there was no apparent interest in hearing from me and no questions about why I was doing what I was doing. It wasn't that I had to cut a couple of minutes of talking points short, it appeared I wasn't going to be allowed to make any statement at all. I was just told to break the record. I had to interrupt the host to get in the message that I was doing this to promote STEM education and that if kids set their mind to a goal and pursue it with a passion, they can accomplish anything. I am proud to this day that I had the frame of mind as well as the courage to interrupt and make my point on live national television.

I then donned the blindfold and did one last quick practice session to make sure I was prepared as Billy Bush said, "now this isn't the real thing yet." The adjudicator checked my blindfold and said, "for the record books, ready, set, go!" I began juggling. I was off to a good start. I felt good, my hands were steady, and I wasn't too nervous. It wasn't my fastest juggling, but I was still on pace to break both the records I was there to break. It was a dream come true and nearly impossible to believe at the same time. I was going to break two Guinness World Records titles on live national television. The moment overwhelmed me. About 15 seconds into the attempt, it was as if a bear jumped out at me. I had one of the biggest adrenaline surges in my life. My heart rate spiked. My blood pressure was off the charts. My arms turned to jelly. I could barely tell where my arms were. My fine motor control was completely gone. My arms started shaking with jerky motions and within a couple of seconds of the adrenaline surge, I dropped a ball.

Did I wonder if something like this might happen, and was I prepared for such a moment?

Yes. Yes, I was. I knew getting nervous and dropping a ball was my biggest risk and had informed the adjudicator I was planning to start the attempt over if I dropped a ball. I had practiced so much; I could tell where the ball had fallen by the sound it made hitting the floor. I reached down and picked it up in one fluid motion without taking off my blindfold. I said confidently, "Here we go!"

I had some adrenaline left in my system, but it was manageable when I started the second time after a "ready, set, go". I wasn't juggling quite as fast at the start, but within a couple of seconds, I was able to settle into a pattern fast enough to break both records. I made it a few seconds longer this time before I had another disabling anxiety attack. The adrenaline surged through my body. My blood pressure spiked. My arms turned to jelly. Within seconds of this crushing wave of adrenaline, I dropped another ball.

This time I didn't have a plan. I reached down to pick up the ball again and my hand hit the floor. I awkwardly patted around on the floor feeling for the ball with my blindfold still on, but my hand came up empty. The TV showed me ducking down to pick up a ball, but it was only from the waist up, so the television frame showed empty space. I had to take off the blindfold to find the ball and pick it up. After I found it, I stood and said "one more time" as I jumped back and forth trying to calm my nerves by burning the adrenaline with motion. I was on live national television. The hosts were looking for approval, and apparently, they got it. I said "too many nerves" as I bounced back and forth.

I was unexpectedly at peace. If you would have asked me in advance how I would have felt if you told me I dropped the ball twice, I would have said terrible. Surprisingly, I didn't fear failure. I still had confidence I could break this record. I began my last attempt on live television. I juggled for five seconds. Then I made it to ten seconds, then fifteen and twenty, and I kept going. It wasn't until the minute was halfway up that my body once again went into a panic attack that turned my arms into bloated, wobbling tendrils that seemed to flop around without direction. This time I fought harder for control. My juggling pace fell dramatically, but I held on. I knew if I could just finish the minute, I would still break the blindfolded speed juggling record. I slowed to an unbearably slow pace and gave up on the overall speed juggling record. I just needed to finish the minute.

Despite my best effort. Despite all the practice, focus, and preparation, I dropped another ball. There was a slight groan. Billy Bush said, "Well, there's a consolation prize, and it's a hug." Billy Bush gave me a light hug and so did Hoda Kotb. I can be seen on the TV smiling large as my head appears over her shoulder. The smile was fake.

The camera cut away and the hosts left for their next set.

I felt surprisingly calm. Perhaps I was in denial. Maybe I was still holding on to hope that it wasn't yet over. I had watched the Guinness World Records specials as a child and they often had a backstage attempt after the show and the person who had failed with the live audience would succeed later in a backstage attempt. I didn't know if that was even a thing on the TODAY show. I don't remember how it came up or who proposed it, but it was determined that they'd find a place to give me another try. There was some confusion about where we could film, what camera we could use, and where it would be displayed for slow-motion review to count the number of catches. We wandered down some stairs and then back up when that location didn't work. I was told by the Guinness World Records team that I was only going to be given one last attempt. I would have been fine with that condition if they just hadn't told me.

We found a space to make one last attempt, and I donned the blindfold to start juggling for an off-air camera on the Guinness adjudicator's cue. I was off to a good start and passed the mark of my first attempt without getting nervous at all. Then I made it to twenty seconds, twenty-five, thirty, thirty-five. Instead of a massive adrenaline rush, I felt myself getting a much smaller dose this time. My arms lost some control, but I could still juggle. At forty seconds I was still juggling, but not fast enough to break the overall speed juggling record. I could still break the blindfolded juggling record, however, and that's what I was now shooting for. I just needed to hang on and finish the minute. At forty-five seconds, I was struggling. My juggling pattern had slowed to what felt like a snail's pace. Then I hit fifty seconds, passing the forty-nine seconds I had juggled when I originally set the record. My arms were mush at this point, and I was desperately trying to maintain the unseen juggling pattern. I was so close to setting my first Guinness World Records title with a live Guinness World Records adjudicator. Just a half-hour before this moment, I had watched the Guinness World Records adjudicator place the certificate with my name on it in the frame. I was seconds away from at least getting to receive it on live TV.

Fifty-two seconds into my final attempt, I dropped the final ball. The stopwatch was stopped, and I hung my head. As I juggled, I was counting and knew I had gotten only about 330 catches. I was only thirty-three short of the record mark and needed only another five seconds even at my slow juggling pace. The adjudicator knew I broke the record in forty-nine seconds previously and said I'd made it fifty-two seconds trying to offer hope that maybe I'd broken the record. I knew there was none. I knew I hadn't broken the record, but there was no way for him to know other than to take my word for it. He said he would count the catches in slow-motion anyway. He had the studio play the footage back in slow-motion. As the footage was played back, I thought about what had just transpired. The adrenaline rush quickly subsided and five minutes later the Guinness World Records adjudicator announced that indeed I was short of the record mark. He waited to see if TODAY would have him back on to announce the last attempt and that it was just short of the mark. Apparently, they had more interesting content to air and they passed on the opportunity to bring him back on set. I made polite conversation, may have held my son, kissed my wife on the cheek, and mindlessly left the studio to catch the limo back to the hotel. The ride wasn't there. The one person around offered to see if they could find someone to arrange a limo, but I declined. I needed the exercise. Jennifer and I walked back to the hotel. I don't remember if we talked.

When we got back to the hotel, we packed up and went from there to a friend's apartment who was going to host us for the rest of the weekend. She was at work, so we dropped our stuff off and put Jeremy down for a nap. I left to go find some groceries for the weekend. By the time I got to the grocery store, the shock and denial were passing. I started to internalize what had happened.

I wandered up and down the grocery store isles putting nothing in my basket. I wanted to cry. I did cry. I was so angry I wanted to rip the merchandise from the shelves and throw it on the floor.

It felt like the biggest failure of my life.

I wanted to crawl in a hole and disappear.

Five million people had seen me fail on live TV, but even worse: all my family, friends, and coworkers would feel sorry for me. I imagined they would try to say nice things like "I wouldn't have even been willing to try that on TV," or "You should be so proud of yourself for just making it," or "I wanted to scream at the host who kept talking while you were trying to juggle." I found out later the hosts were talking while I was juggling and were making up fake catch counts. I don't remember hearing them while I was on set, and it did not influence me. My friends were sure it did and tried to make excuses for me. These well-meaning comments and excuses would not make me feel any better.

I put on my best face and acted like I was doing okay, and you know what? It sort of worked. I made fun of the situation. I told folks that I now had my best failure story to inspire others to overcome their failures. And I did. I told that story and people responded. When some people who hear the story found out it had just happened a couple of months before, they weren't sure I could be over it yet. In truth, I wasn't. But in every telling, I felt a little better. The sting became less painful. Almost two years later, I would still cringe when watching the footage, but at least the memory of the pain had faded.

I may have failed, but I learned that failure isn't permanent. In the moment, I felt like I never wanted to put myself out there again because the pain was so profound. But failure is only permanent when you believe it is. Failure is only permanent when you give up. Instead of acting like I had the biggest failure of my life, I acted like I didn't. I acted like it was just a temporary setback and didn't dwell on the pain and the negative emotions. I have found that people take their cues on your failure from you, and if you act like you haven't had a devastating personal failure, they tend not to think of it as such. Instead of giving up, I went out and set more Guinness World Records titles and I haven't stopped since. I played the part of being strong until I became strong.

I do not let the fear of failure stop me, even though I can and do fail. You shouldn't let the fear of failure stop you either. The biggest failure I could have imagined happened to me and was seen by more people than I thought may see me again for the rest of my life. But that didn't have to stop me, and I didn't let it. If I had let the fear of failure stop me. I would never have had that experience. If I had let the memory of that failure stop me, I would have broken only a fraction of the Guinness World Records titles that I have today. Since I didn't give up, many more experiences I never could have imagined have presented themselves.

Most Juggling Catches in 1 Minute Blindfolded (3 Balls)
Previous Record: 363 catches
Best Attempt: ~330 catches in 52 seconds

11
ASK FOR HELP

Longest Duration Balancing a Bicycle on the Chin
Previous Record: 2 minutes 1.45 Seconds

I didn't want to have to tell people for long that my latest Guinness World Records title attempt was a failure, so I quickly set out to break another one. Ashrita Furman had the distinction of holding the Guinness World Records title for most titles currently held. We also have overlapping skill sets. I saw a video in which Ashrita broke the record for the longest duration balancing a bicycle on the chin and decided I should give it a try. It was right up my alley after setting the chainsaw chin balancing record.

When I received the rules, I discovered the minimum weight of the bike was 27 pounds and that it had to be balanced either from the seat or a wheel. The first thing I did was weigh my bikes at home. My highly accurate scale tops out at 32 pounds, and my mountain bike maxed it out when I was still supporting a substantial amount of the weight. I weighed my road bike, and it also maxed out my scale meaning it was far heavier than the minimum weight as well. My wife's bike weighed a little less but still maxed out the scale. I wasn't going to use any of them for the official attempt, but I decided I could use them for practice.

I tried only once to balance the wheel of the bike on my chin. I couldn't even figure out how to hold it upright by the wheel without it tipping over. I almost smashed my hand between the wheel and the frame by the brakes as my bike spun to the ground while I held the wheel with my hand. After that, I only balanced it from the seat. Adopting the right strategy makes success a lot easier.

There are a couple of difficult parts to this record: The first is building up the neck strength to keep a 27+ pound object balanced on the chin for over 2 minutes. I was sure I would be able to do that with enough training. My main concern was that once the bike was on my chin, the handlebars would rotate side to side and if there was a large weight shift, it could throw off the balance. With such a heavy object, the risk of injury to myself or others was much higher than smaller objects were it to tumble off my chin. No structural modifications could be made to the bike, so there was no legal way for me to lock the handlebars. I found that if I turned the handlebars to the side before placing it on my chin, it solved my problem.

While lifting the bike onto my chin, the handlebars would often swing back and forth. Once balanced on my chin, the handlebars settled into their lowest potential energy point. They then only moved slightly as I made minor adjustments to keep the bike balanced.

I needed to find a bike that weighed just over 27 pounds without adding or removing any parts. I considered scouring Craigslist for likely candidates but realized it would take way too much time: both mine and the poor sellers' who would meet me simply to have me weigh the bike and say it was too light or too heavy. I also considered a second-hand store but didn't want to buy a bike I was only going to use for this one activity and never ride. I decided I would ask for help from the most likely source I could find: a bike shop.

I contacted Ken of Ken's bicycle warehouse to ask if I could borrow a bike. As a child, my dad bought my first mountain bike from him, and in high school, I got my second from him after the first was stolen. I also bought a unicycle from him between my eighth- and ninth-grade years to add to my junior high talent show act. Ken could not only save me the cost of buying a bike but could also point me to likely candidates, so I didn't have to weigh them all trying to find one that was the correct weight. Ken proved very helpful.

Ken agreed to have me come to the shop and borrow a bike. He pointed me to a smaller women's model he expected to be just over 27 pounds. I put my scale on the ground and weighed the bike on it. It rang in at just over 23 pounds. I said we needed a heavier bike. Fortunately, Ken knows his bikes. When he said a bike 'should' weigh just over 27 pounds, he knew it did. He didn't trust my scale. I realized that I had put it down on the carpet. It was the hard-industrial carpet you might find in a highly trafficked office building or a bike shop, but it was still carpet and my scale required compression to determine weight. If the carpet was absorbing any of that compression with its short feet not keeping the body from touching the underlying carpet, it would give an inaccurately, low reading. I moved the scale to the tile floor and weighed the bike again. It was 29 pounds. I thanked Ken profusely for both letting me borrow the bike and for making sure I got one that was the right weight.

I signed up for Meridian's "Talent Tournament" held at a local park. Two dozen acts were competing for votes from the spectators in September at the Meridian Block Party. I had less than a week to practice with my newly borrowed bike, but I didn't suspect that this new equipment would be a problem. The biggest issue was building up my neck, back, and jaw strength to support that much weight for that long without injury, and I had already been doing that for some time. Avoiding injury was my biggest concern. I could put the bike on my chin and break the record at any given moment, but in doing so, I could risk seriously throwing out my neck or back. Without proper muscle support, I could do serious damage and might end up with a very sore back or worse. Fortunately, I had been practicing with my heavier bikes and my weights at home.

I built up neck strength with a bicep curl bar at home. I put weights on one end and a tennis ball on the other. An X-slit in the tennis ball allowed the end of the bar that rests on my chin to slide into the ball protecting my chin from the metal. The weights were placed on the other end of the bar that was lifted into the air. I increased the weight and duration in practice sessions over several weeks. If I used too much weight or balanced the weight too long, my lower back would bruise and feel sore the next day. I'd have to take a couple of days off and scale back the weight and duration and slow the progression. During the first practice sessions, my jaw muscles were often the sorest, but they quickly became accustomed to the weight. After weeks of practice, my neck muscles were the ones that would lock up first during training and would be the main reason I'd want to stop a training run. For as much as my neck muscles hurt during practice, they were rarely sore the next day. My lower back was always the largest concern. It rarely hurt during practice, but my compressed spine would be the most debilitating that night and the next day if I practiced with too much weight or for too long.

By the time I got the bike, my neck, back, and jaw were up for the challenge. I practiced with the new bike to get a feel for its motions, how it reacted to balancing corrections, and where to focus my eyes while balancing it.

On the Saturday morning of the Meridian Block Party, I packed up my bag of juggling equipment and strapped the bike onto my car bike rack. The event was set up as a talent contest with 16 acts performing simultaneously for two hours. I decided to put up signs advertising the record attempt 1.5 hours into the event. I should have just done it right at the start. Street performing is a fickle activity. I have learned that you need a crowd to draw a crowd. Once you have someone's attention, other people naturally get curious to find out what's going on. They come to watch which begets more watching. Conversely, little attention begets less attention. I could be doing the most amazingly technical juggling in the world, and if people are walking by ignoring it, other people will follow that cue and walk by as well. Some may look at what's going on as they walk by, but few will stop and watch unless invited. If you have a crowd of people and are doing a simple trick that doesn't require much skill, other people will stop and watch as well simply because there's already a crowd.

I planned to do several mini acts culminating with the Guinness World Records title attempt act. I began to gather a crowd at the start of my first act. I was the only act actively trying to gather a crowd and quickly had dozens of people watching. I did some 3-ball juggling and then 4- and 5-ball juggling. I hyped the bike balance record and even balanced the bike on my chin for a few seconds to give the folks a taste and concluded with knife juggling on a balance board.

Each member of the audience was given three stones to distribute into bins of their favorite acts to vote for the winner. I received several stones and let the crowd disperse. If I had been the only act, or performing for money, I would have tried hard to keep some of that crowd around as a seed crowd for the next act. I would have said that I was about to start again soon so if you joined late, stick around for the next act that would be unique and exciting. Instead, since there were 15 other acts, many largely being ignored (especially the ones nearest me), I turned off my mic and took a break. I would not have a crowd even half that large for the rest of the day, even when I was attempting to break the Guinness World Records title.

The team of witnesses and timekeepers showed up about a half-hour before the time scheduled for the record attempt and we went over the paperwork and rules. The bike was weighed, and we set up a big clock so the audience could track the record progress. I made an announcement that the record attempt was going to begin, started all the video cameras, and placed the bike on my chin.

I knew I had a tight space for the balancing act but didn't realize just how tight it was going to feel. I was stationed near two benches that were bolted to the ground. The open area behind them was only a few feet wide and backed up to a three-foot-tall metal fence that protected the six-foot drop-off into a pond. If I were to touch the fence or a bench with my legs or body, the attempt would be disqualified.

As I balanced the bike on my chin, it shifted ever so slightly, and I had to shuffle my feet to stay under it. I kept shuffling more than planned and within a minute I was perilously close to the pond fence. I wasn't sure how close I was, as I was staring up, but I knew it couldn't be very far away. This resulted in me keeping my body stationary and trying to lean just my neck and head toward the fence to bring the bike back under my body. This technique didn't work out well since the bike was so heavy. Since I was only leaning and couldn't get far enough under it, I kept shuffling toward the fence. About 1 minute 30 seconds into the first attempt, just 30 seconds shy of the record, I felt the fence with my waist. I heard a gasp from the crowd, and the bike started falling off my chin over the fence toward the pond. I was barely able to grab the bike with my hands and reel it in before it made the long drop into the water. The attempt had failed. I was relieved the borrowed bike hadn't fallen into the pond, but the attempt was unsuccessful. I didn't want to give up just yet, but my neck was far too tired for another attempt right away.

I decided I would take a ten-minute break and try again on the other side of the benches. I had to clear out what audience I had to make a bigger space and reposition my cameras and the clock. When practicing, I would limit myself to one long practice run per day with the full weight, so I wasn't sure how prepared I would be to try a second-long run with only a few minutes break. I was expecting adrenaline and the sure knowledge of a couple weeks' rest to get me through.

I once again swung the wheels into the air and put the bike seat onto my chin. I positioned it with the center of gravity directly above my chin and released the bike with my hands. The clock was started, and I had 2 minutes 1.45 seconds to go. I made it to 1 minute without incident, but my neck was getting sore fast. At 1 minute 30 seconds, my muscles were on fire but still holding. Since I had more space to move, I didn't try to jut my neck out without moving my feet and body under the bike when it shifted. The result of allowing myself to shuffle a little more was that I ended up having to shuffle around a lot less. At a minute and 45 seconds, I started to wobble just a little but knew I was going to make it. As the two-minute mark approached, I was laser-focused so as not to mess up in the last few seconds. I passed the record mark, and those watching cheered. I kept going. Now that the pressure was off, I could focus on extending the record while maintaining good form. At 2 minutes 20 seconds, I didn't think I could last much longer. Ten seconds later, I started raising my hands to grab the bike. At 2 minutes 36 seconds my neck was a frozen fire of needles. I pulled the bike off my chin and began to celebrate.

It took me two tries, but in the end, the attempt was successful. I had to practice for months using the resources I had, but to make this attempt a success I needed to find and ask for help.

I could have tried to source the bike on my own, but it was way more efficient to consult an expert who could not only direct me to exactly what I needed but also provide it for no cost (other than a post to social media and a big thank you). While another approach would have worked, asking for help saved me a lot of time and effort. I advocate for having a growth mindset - this idea that you can get better at anything. But many times, you don't need to get better at something when there are experts who can do it for you, and it's a skill you'll never need again. (I'm not talking about math.) And if you do want to learn something new, often the best way to get better at something is to watch the experts do it first. In my case, I used an expert to find the right bike since it was something I was unlikely to need to do again. I also watched the bike-balancing expert Ashrita

Furman to learn an effective bike-balancing technique. Learning from, imitating, and finally improving upon knowledge from an expert, is an excellent way to improve at almost anything.

Longest Duration Balancing a Bicycle on the Chin
Previous Record: 2 minutes 1.45 seconds
New Record: 2 minutes 36 seconds

12

KEEP MOVING, ESPECIALLY WHEN YOU WANT TO STOP

Greatest Distance Walked on Foot
Balancing a Pool Cue on One Finger
Previous Record: 14.4 kilometers (8.9 miles)

So much of life is about momentum. Where is yours taking you? Newton's First Law of Motion states, "A body at rest will remain at rest, and a body in motion will remain in motion unless it is acted upon by an external force." What forces are acting on you? And what forces do you need to generate to move toward your goals? Do you feel like you're stuck, unmoving, or maybe even moving the wrong direction?

The first thing you must do when pursuing your life's goals is to get started. You have to get yourself in motion pursuing your goals. Much of America is in motion but not pursuing any growth. We go to work and come home to a couch to watch TV or scroll through our Facebook or TikTok feed. Maybe we have the same beer with the same friend and have the same conversation every time. Maybe we participate in our weekly softball game, book club, Bible study, or lunch with friends, but we do it without thoughtful purpose. We haven't thought through what we want to accomplish from those experiences. Some forces will make you want to quit a purposeful goal, including pain, disillusionment, laziness, criticism, lack of belief, lack of motivation, or competing priorities. To maximize the impact and benefits, we have to break out of this habit (nonproductive momentum) and think about our purpose. The purpose may be to deepen interpersonal relationships or relieve stress, but if you don't know why you're doing what you're doing, you may not be getting what you want from it. Once you're in motion and going the right direction, it's a lot easier to keep going.

I decided I wanted to break the Guinness World Records title for greatest distance walked while balancing a pool cue on one finger. One of the first things I did was buy a pool cue from a thrift shop. It didn't meet the Guinness World Records specifications for length and weight, but at least I could start practicing with it. I could have made an excuse of not finding a cue that met the Guinness World Records specifications to not get started, which would have shown both laziness and lack of motivation. I did not. Then I had to practice. I would go on walks with my wife, and I'd bring the cue along and balance it on one finger as we traveled around the neighborhood (sorry, and thank you, Jennifer!). I then went on runs and realized I could quickly cover a lot more ground while running. I contacted Guinness World Records since most of the distance records were the greatest distance traveled on foot instead of the greatest distance walked. They agreed running could be allowed and updated the rules.

I practiced for weeks and the weeks turned into months. When I first started practicing, I would only run on tracks where I could focus my full attention on the cue and not have to worry about where I was going or what I might step on. As I got better, I ran varied routes with uneven ground, then on sidewalks and across streets. I got good enough at balancing the cue while running that I could safely look both directions before crossing a street while still maintaining the balance. It has always been a goal of mine to not get run over by a car. On one particularly harrowing 9-mile run in New York City, I realized that the drivers there are less forgiving of pedestrians than in Boise. I decided to exercise more caution in my practice runs. I got used to people giving me weird looks and decided I couldn't let myself be embarrassed. Sometimes when I walked or ran with others, they would be embarrassed for me. One time I hiked up to the top of the hill known as Table Rock in the Boise foothills with a group of friends with the cue on my finger, and they couldn't help but apologize for me to the people we passed.

The existing record was 14.4 km (8.9 miles) which is equivalent to 36 laps around a 400-meter track. I wanted to do something a little more exciting than jog around a track and contacted a local half marathon. FitOne is a charity event supporting the St Luke's Children's hospital.

Since I promote STEM education, often with the focus on kids pursuing it, there was some initial hesitation with a partnership. The hospital treats many children who are terminally ill. During treatment, they focus on kids living their lives to the fullest right now and avoid focusing on the future. We agreed that any message related to STEM should be focused on the doctors and nurses who help care for the children and the technology that improves care.

The next challenge was to gather all the evidence required by Guinness World Records to document the attempt. The rules state that the entire event needs to be captured on camera from a static location. Since I was going to be running a 13-mile course, this was impossible (or highly impractical to secure the necessary footage from a geosynchronous satellite or hovering helicopter). I contacted Guinness World Records asking if I could have the witnesses accompany me for the entire run instead of providing the video evidence from a static location. They said it would be fine if the witnesses were with me the entire time to validate the attempt. This wasn't clear enough language since they would go on to request video footage from the entire event anyway. They assumed moving footage; I assumed the witnesses would be enough. They have since clarified their language and video footage is always required for the entire attempt. I decided I should have at least three people with me at all times, in case something happened to one like a twisted ankle or some other injury where a witness couldn't keep up. I was also hoping they could help provide a human shield from other runners if necessary. I would also need help getting food and water since diverting my attention from the cue balance for even a moment to pick up a cup of water was risky.

These last few points are very important. The cue had to be balanced on one finger the entire time. It could not fall off, switch fingers, touch another part of the body, or touch any other object. If it did, the record attempt ended at that moment. I could be 8.8 miles into the attempt, and if an overhead tree branch brushed the cue, the record attempt would be over and disqualified.

The hardest part of balancing a cue isn't the balancing or the running. I had that down. The hardest part was trying to do some other activity while balancing the cue, like grabbing a glass of water, drinking it, and setting it down. If I ever switched my focus to independently moving my left hand for some task, the cue balance on my right hand would falter. If you want to get a feel for what I mean, try drawing a sideways figure 8 in the air with your right index finger. It's not too hard. I bet you can do it down with virtually no difficulty, and you could probably keep it up indefinitely. Now while doing that, try to draw a vertical number 8 with your left hand. Whatever you do, don't stop the figure 8 with your right hand for even an instant, or you drop the cue! In the same way, even simple tasks with my left hand were risky.

Much of the route of the half marathon was along a foot and bike path in Boise, known as the Greenbelt. It is a wonderful, highly utilized recreation and commuting path that extends for dozens of miles on either side of the Boise River. Appropriately, much of it is pleasantly shaded by overhanging trees in the city whose name means "the city of trees." These trees are regularly pruned so as not to interfere with pedestrians and cyclists, but the pruners don't appear to have ever considered that an over six-foot-tall runner carrying a four-foot pool cue might want to run under those same trees. Given the frequency of such an occurrence, it was obvious I was going to have to be the one to adapt instead of the pruners.

I recruited three witnesses, all of whom decided they'd run the full distance with me (though I felt bad because I unintentionally misrepresented how fast I was going to run).

The course officially measured in at 12.93 miles after a late course change due to flooding along the Boise River, so it wasn't a full half marathon. I didn't need the last 0.2 miles to break the record anyway, I just needed the first 8.9 miles (or last 8.9 if I had a drop within the first 4 miles). If I dropped the cue between 4 miles and 8.9 miles on the course, I would not be able to break the record.

On the morning of the attempt, I met my witness team at the start line. It was cool, but not too chilly, which was important since I wasn't allowed to wear gloves. I drank very little that morning and tried to go to the bathroom at least seven times before the race started since there was no fitting into a porta-potty during the run with a cue balanced on one finger.

The race started with the gun at 7:30 AM. A thousand runners made their way across the crowded start line shortly after and I wasn't one of them. I decided to start about a minute after the last runner of the main pack so I could avoid the congested traffic at the start. I would catch up to the main pack of people anyway and before I finished, we would weave through and pass about 700 of the 1,000 runners during the race.

I had recruited Jeremy, a friend of mine, as the official photographer and videographer, so he was sent ahead to capture the start of the race for both the main pack and then for me a few minutes later. After the main pack was well past the start line I took off, and within five minutes I had caught up to the back of the main pack of runners. While it was slow work finding the holes in the crowd to maneuver through, it was helpful to regulate my pace and kept me from running too fast. One of the biggest risks during this attempt was fatigue. When tired, I'm much more likely to stumble, lose the cue balance, or miss dodging a low-hanging tree branch. Since I was forced to go slowly early on, my legs and body were fresh and strong for longer.

The four of us running all wore stickers on our backs identifying that a Guinness World Records title attempt was taking place. There were lots of fun comments: "You're my hero," shout-outs, and "NO WAY!" And of course, there's always one or two who aren't enjoying the run anyway and enjoy less being passed by a guy balancing a pool cue on a finger. One poor guy was especially miffed when he was behind us and our group came across the low-hanging trees on the Greenbelt. It required me to slow down so I could bend low enough to get my finger less than two feet off the ground to get safely under the tree branch. This required me to slow to a walk, and he had to run around and pass the group a couple of times just to have me pass him back a minute later. I'll admit it was a minor inconvenience for him, but I'm pretty sure he was mostly upset that a guy could run faster than him while balancing a cue on a finger.

I also ran much of the race with a Boise High School junior. She was running the race at about the same pace as me and apparently thought it was cool to run next to a guy setting a Guinness World Records title. I enjoyed our conversation, but I never actually saw her face. When looking through the pictures after the race, it wasn't hard to figure out who she was. She had photobombed several of the pictures taken for Guinness World Records verification with some funny faces and even cut right into the video of me passing the current record at the 9-mile mark on the course.

I was a little worried about getting nervous and shaking so much that the cue might bounce off my finger as I approached the current record. I ought not to have been worried. The problem of shaking with nerves arises when too much adrenaline enters the system. When I'm speed juggling, my arms are active and the rest of me isn't doing much. Exercise burns off adrenaline and running is a lot more exercise than just my arms moving for speed juggling. Any extra adrenaline that entered my system was quickly used during a half marathon before it built up enough to affect my arms.

Once I passed the record mark of 8.9 miles, I decided it was time to speed up as I no longer needed to run conservatively. I had passed more than half the race participants already, but I was still running more slowly than even an easy pace at my fitness level. I ran faster. I felt good. The cue balance was solid. After we merged onto a street with a lot more space to pass runners than the narrow Greenbelt, I ran even faster. For the last couple of miles, I let the afterburners fly and made the accidental speed expectation deception to my witnesses known. I had told them I was planning on running a 2-hour 15-minute to 2-hour 30-minute race and instead finished in under two hours. That's shaving 1-2 minutes per mile which wasn't fair to my witnesses. Two were training for other races and didn't plan for this to be a hard run. One was recovering from injury. None of them complained before or after, but I still feel a little bad.

I made it 12.93 miles in about 1 hour 58 minutes without a single drop.

The metaphorical drops wouldn't come until later when additional evidence including footage from the entire race was requested by Guinness World Records. It took over a year, an additional letter from the race director, 60 additional video snippets and pictures, and a lot of patience, but in the end, the record was finally approved.

It started with an idea. I wanted to break a world record, but I needed to get started. I bought a cue to start practicing even though it didn't meet the Guinness World Records specifications. I could have found excuses not to practice or even try, but instead, I made time to practice. I got myself into motion and once I started, I didn't let life stop my momentum. I practiced until I proved to myself I could break the record. Then I went ahead and practiced until I was sure I would break it. I broke the record with 8.9 miles of running and tacked on nearly an additional 50%. So much of life is about momentum. Where is yours taking you?

Greatest Distance Travelled on Foot
Balancing a Pool Cue on One Finger
Previous Record 14.4 kilometers (8.9 miles)
New record: 12.93 miles

13
THINK OF THE BRAIN AS A MUSCLE

Longest Duration Balancing a Ladder on the Chin
Previous Record: 4 minutes 9 seconds

In the collective psyche of our current culture, there is a myth that the human brain is only changeable when we're children. Phrases have entered our lexicon like "you can't teach an old dog new tricks." We lament not learning a second language as children as if the opportunity has escaped us forever. We talk about the pliability of a child's brain and note how quickly and effortlessly they grow. We comment on every little new skill they've learned since yesterday or last week. We see this change so readily in children, but at some point, as they grow, we stop seeing it. When a person reaches adulthood, they are not only expected to be responsible and in control, but we expect them to stop learning new skills as rapidly.

This perception is false, and there's proof.

The brain should be thought of like a muscle that can learn and grow. The more you work it, the stronger it gets. When kids are learning, they're working their brains hard all the time learning new things every day. They don't know any better since everything requires effort. At some point, we start getting good at a lot of things. When those things aren't as hard anymore, we start comparing the things we're good at with the things we're not. We become comfortable not working as hard. When we do face a challenge, instead of working hard to get through it, we make excuses about how that's not our "gifting." This is just an excuse not to try. If we were willing to be more like children, face every new challenge as a part of life, and have the mindset we could overcome it, we'd be able to accomplish a lot more.

In Carol Dweck's *Mindset*, she documents that adults, when primed with a growth mindset, learn much more readily than those with a fixed mindset. Priming people with a growth mindset involves informing them that a test or task that they're practicing for can result in dramatic improvement with studying or practice. Or sometimes, more generically, that any test or task can be improved upon with work. When people believe they can learn a new skill or gain more knowledge, learning either becomes their goal, or they realize that effort makes them stronger. In either case, they spend more time working hard and achieving more.

Time and time again I have been able to learn a new skill. Knowing that I can learn any new skill is paramount when teaching it to myself. When I first try something new, I usually fail. And then I fail again. And then I fail some more. I fail so often and so consistently that it's sometimes all I seem to do. But I keep consciously trying - especially when I'm practicing where other people can see me. Physiologists have documented that about the age of 5, kids generally develop self-awareness and shame. This shame is what keeps up from doing things that are frowned upon by others be it licking our plate at the dinner table, going potty with the door open, asking personal questions in public, or committing a social faux pas. Looking silly in public by trying and failing to complete an activity is a faux pas and results in discomfort, so most of us actively avoid it. I must overcome this aversion quickly to learn new skills.

When I'm trying to break a Guinness World Records title, I'm trying to beat the best in the world at something I may not yet know how to do. Part of me says I should just give up because it's not possible. But if I keep up with it, I invariably improve. I get better at whatever I'm practicing and get closer and closer to breaking a world record. If I spend enough time, energy, and effort, I can become the best in the world at anything (while noting that if the best in the world has spent thousands of hours on that single skill, it will probably also take me thousands of hours to catch up and overtake them).

When I was in college, I decided I wanted to learn how to balance objects on my chin. Balancing is a natural complement to juggling. It didn't go well at first, but after tens of hours of practice over several months, I got pretty good at it. My objective was to increase the repertoire of acts I had at my disposal for juggling performances. As with many performance art activities, the hardest acts to perform are often not the most impressive to watch, and the most impressive acts are often easier to master. Balancing a juggling club on the chin while juggling is quite difficult, but not as visually impressive as the easier task of balancing an 8-foot A-frame ladder on the chin without juggling. I often take a 6- or 8-foot A-frame ladder and give the audience a choice: should I balance it on my chin while it's open? or while it's closed? To set up the act, I ask the audience to cheer more loudly for the option they prefer. I start with the closed option, offering it in a muted monotone voice. I then do a spectacular showmanship buildup dramatically yelling the option to balance the ladder while it's open as I throw the legs apart. The audience invariably takes the bait and the open option always gets the louder cheer. The twist is that at the end, after the loud cheering for open dies down enough to be heard, I deadpan, "Closed it is." The audience loves it, but it's not a particularly difficult act to perform (nor did I create it).

Ten years later, I discovered that there is a Guinness World Records title for the longest duration balancing a ladder on the chin. I could already balance a ladder on my chin, the challenge now was to do it for over four minutes. I needed to build muscle strength to sustain the balance for minutes versus the seconds I do in a live performance. I needed to push my muscles to the point where they were challenged and stretched and got little micro-tears that would then be filled in by new muscle tissue. I would increase the volume and strength of the muscles in my neck, back, jaw, and legs this way. It's well understood that when you work out a muscle it gets stronger. Challenging a muscle is painful as it gets stretched and pushed. Working muscle results in the lactic acid buildup that leaves it sore. Right after a workout, the muscles are fatigued, torn, and temporarily weaker needing time to recover. But with time to heal and the proper nutrition, the muscles end up stronger as the torn muscle is filled with the new muscle fiber. I put objects on my chin and balanced them for longer and longer and got heavier and heavier things to build up the strength in my neck, back, jaw, and legs. I challenged them to grow and stretch beyond what they were previously capable of doing. I accepted the pain, discomfort, and temporary weakening of my muscles because I knew in the end, they would be stronger.

The brain should be thought about similarly. The mechanisms are different, but the brain, like a muscle, can learn and grow. It doesn't gain muscle fiber as it's stretched, but it does grow new neural connections between different parts of the brain as it's challenged with learning new activities. As you learn new skills or practice old ones in more challenging ways, new connections are created. If you've ever watched a child for more than a few days trying new things, the progress is obvious. They didn't previously have a skill, but after trying, failing, and then failing and trying again, they get closer to and better at learning new skills. But new learning isn't limited to children. It's just that a child isn't afraid of failure since it's mostly what they know. It isn't until about the age of 5 that humans develop a sense of self-awareness that results in the fear of judgment of failure by others. When kindergarteners are trying something new and they fail, at some point, they start letting that fear stop them from trying again. We can't let our fear of judgment stop us from trying something new, or we'll stop learning. We need to push and stretch our brains beyond what they're currently capable of doing. We need to challenge our brains until they realize they need to develop new connections to be able to complete a new task. The brain then needs time to recover after being fatigued. It needs proper nutrition to fuel its recovery and plenty of sleep where many of the new connections are consolidated and reinforced. If the brain isn't challenged, it won't develop those essential new neural connections. You have to keep in mind that challenging the brain is uncomfortable and results in fatigue. Just like working out a muscle is uncomfortable and results in fatigue. We already know that lifting weights results in discomfort that means the muscles are being worked hard and the fatigue will pass when the muscles are reinforced and healed. This knowledge results in our willingness to go to the gym and put ourselves through the pain of lifting weights, knowing we'll grow stronger. If you realize the same thing about your brain and working on a new skill, you're more likely to keep up through the pain and fatigue since mental pain and fatigue are signs of progress being made, not of your lack of talent or skill.

We can develop new skills at any age. It isn't that the adult brain stagnates and loses its pliability as we age, we just become accustomed to no longer challenging and stretching it beyond its current limits. In the short term, challenging our brains is uncomfortable. It taxes our system, and additionally, could lead to a failure that may be judged by others. This makes us uncomfortable, and we're predisposed to avoid discomfort. If we look past that discomfort and think of our brains as a muscle, that discomfort can be overcome and not only viewed as necessary, but sought-after. Many athletes seek the thrill of pushing their limits in training since they know they're getting closer to their goal with every uncomfortable step.

After a few months of building up my neck strength, I was ready to break this record. I needed to find a ladder that met the Guinness World Records requirements. It needed to be a minimum of 8 feet tall and weigh more than 7 kilograms or about 15.5 pounds. The issue I ran into was that any ladder I could find that was over 8 feet tall was well over 7 kilograms, and often twice that heavy. After several trips to different hardware stores toting my scale, I found an 8-foot aluminum A-frame later that only weighed 21 pounds. I visited with the manager asking if I could borrow it for a couple of days and bring it back in like-new condition. He had no issue with that plan so long as I paid for it in the meantime and brought it back for a return with the receipt. It was over 5 pounds heavier than required, but it was the lightest ladder I could find over 8 feet tall.

I was invited to come to talk at a middle school assembly in Emmett, Idaho. I made the 45-minute drive out on a sunny afternoon with the ladder strapped to the top of my car.

My uncle was superintendent of the school district, and I had volunteered to come out a few months earlier and talk to the entire district staff about the power of a growth mindset. That presentation had gone well. The middle school decided their students could benefit from the same message and brought me out to speak to 570 of their students.

I had a 45-minute presentation replete with juggling, balancing, and inspirational stories. My life isn't so extraordinary, which is what makes it accessible to so many students. I grew up in a household with about the median household income in America (a little less when I was very young and a little higher by the time I was in high school). I went to public schools from kindergarten through my senior year of high school (except for first grade when my mother homeschooled me). I was in normal classes in primary school and didn't get into the gifted program when I tried out in second grade. I also didn't qualify for the chess team when I tried out in second grade, even though I only needed to survive ten legal moves against the teacher who ran the club. I worked hard and got into both in fifth grade. There was no secret into me getting into MIT other than years of working hard to do well in school, volunteering regularly, staying committed to soccer and other extracurricular activities, and not giving up when I faced setbacks.

I let the kids know they had a bright future ahead of them and they didn't need to go to MIT to succeed. They could do that right where they were by applying themselves to whatever they set out to do.

I then showed that with commitment and effort, they could even do something as cool as or cooler than breaking a Guinness World Records title. I put the ladder on my chin and balanced it in front of 570 middle school students. The group went completely silent.

The first minute was fairly comfortable. The second minute started to get uncomfortable, especially in the back of my neck. By the third minute, under normal circumstances, I would have called it a day and taken the ladder of my chin. When I got to four minutes, I was sweating, the muscles in the back of my neck were cramping, and my jaw was on fire. I wanted to quit. I only had nine seconds more to go to break the record and at four minutes, I was sure I could do it. Since it was local middle school students and I felt confident in my ability to break the record, I didn't feel as much pressure and didn't get as nervous. As the last few seconds ticked by, the anticipation in the room grew. The time elapsed was displayed on the digital scoreboard in the gym, so all the students knew when the current record would be broken. There was no specific request for them to be quiet, but most must have assumed they should, and they were effective at self-policing. When I passed the Guinness World Records-mark of four minutes nine seconds, the students burst out into spontaneous cheers. Who knew 570 middle school students could be so loud? The noise was ear-splitting, and I soaked it in and raised my arms above my head. I was careful to keep my hands away from the ladder so it would be obvious I wasn't touching it, ending the attempt. After a few seconds of cheering, the self-policing started again. They realized if they were trying not to distract me, they should probably keep it up until I was done. In truth, it didn't matter to me.

After five and a half minutes, the pain was immense, and I decided I was done. While I could have continued, I had already broken the record by a substantial margin, and I didn't want to risk injury. As I removed the ladder from my chin, the kids erupted in cheers again, even more loudly this time. I set the ladder down and raised my arms in triumph. Later, a teacher joked that two Guinness World Records titles had been broken: one for the longest time to balance a ladder, and another for the longest time for 570 middle schoolers to remain quiet.

In my adult life, I learned the new skill of balancing objects on my chin. I failed at first, but as the neural connections were formed in my brain, I got better at the activity. The brain is like a muscle that was challenged, stretched, and grew - just like I challenged, stretched, and grew the muscles in my neck, back, jaw, and legs that were necessary to balance a ladder on my chin for over five minutes. In our culture, we know we can grow bigger, faster, and stronger muscles with effort, but somewhere along the way, we forgot we can grow new talents, skills, and abilities with mental effort. We stop applying mental effort and conflate a lack of learning and progress with the lack of learning ability. The formula is simple – if we challenge our brains, we will learn new skills. Think of the incredible possibilities this creates for you.

Longest Duration Balancing a Ladder on the Chin
Previous Record: 4 minutes 9 Seconds
New Record: 5 minutes 32 Seconds

14

THE BRAIN IS MALLEABLE

Longest Duration Blindfolded Juggling (3 Balls)
Previous Record: 6 minutes 34 seconds (held by me)

From the moment I broke my first Guinness World Records title for Longest Duration Blindfolded Juggling, I knew I would break it again. On my first attempt, I was so excited as I approached the record mark that when the audience finally cheered as I passed it, an adrenaline surge caused me to lose fine motor control. A ball sailed long, and the record was only advanced by 5 seconds. I knew I could do better.

An opportunity presented itself exactly one year later. Cradlepoint was hosting its annual block party on the Basque Block in Boise again, and after a year of breaking other Guinness World Records titles, I thought it fitting that I should re-break the first one at the same event where it all started. But what would have happened if I hadn't tried to break a world record in the first place?

In *My Stroke of Insight*, brain scientist Dr. Jill Bolte Taylor documents her experience of having a stroke - literally having parts of her brain die and the multi-year recovery process. She forgot how to talk, walk, think, and do. The parts of the brain that controlled many of those functions were deprived of oxygen so long that they died. Those dead parts of the brain would never recover. But the brain is changeable, malleable, and an extraordinarily adaptable organ. The parts of the brain can change and adapt to meet a need much like a soccer midfield player can play forward if additional offense is needed or move back if additional defense is required. If a red card removes a player from the game, the change can become permanent. Dr. Taylor rewired her brain to have different parts of it take over the functions that she had lost. The most profound realization for me as I read her book wasn't that someone who had a stroke could rewire their brain, which is quite remarkable; the most remarkable realization was that anyone can rewire their brain with enough effort and perseverance.

The effort required to rewire your brain isn't like the effort required to rewire a house. You don't need a design layout and schematics to understand how it is going to look at the end. What you need instead is to have a vision of what you would like to be able to do, how you'd like to be able to act or react, or what you want to accomplish. Then you start trying to do those things. If you have a goal in mind and start working toward it with deliberate and regular practice, the process of rewiring will happen naturally. It will not, however, happen immediately. The brain takes time to adapt and respond to new actions or thinking processes. Over time it will adapt, and you will get better and faster at new things as they become familiar.

When you learn a new skill, the brain is forming new connections. You create new neurons through a process called neurogenesis. Until recently, scientists didn't think adults could grow new neurons, but this misconception has been refuted since new ways to scan the brain have been developed. These scans revealed adults regularly create new neurons. You have neurons all over the brain that fire to send messages to different parts of the brain. Once you've learned a new skill, something else starts to happen as you practice. When you have a connection in the brain and use it over and over by practicing (especially deliberate practice), myelin sheaths form around the neurons to protect the signals and make them pass more quickly and reliably. When the neuron fires for the umpteenth time after much practice, the sheath around it is so strong the signal is received quickly and in full force. When we perform a skill naturally, almost without thinking, we've developed what has been dubbed in our culture "muscle memory." It is more accurate to call it neuron memory as it's these neuron connections and the myelin sheaths that are doing all the "remembering."

A myelin sheath is a protective wrapping around a neural pathway. To start, a neural connection is much like a porous hose that transports water. Much of the water is lost through the holes in the hose as it travels and while some of the signal gets to the end, it is slowed and not all of it reaches its destination. As you use the neural pathway more, by repeating the action, the sheath forms. The sheath is analogous to wrapping a porous hose that loses water with a covering to plug the holes. The result of wrapping the tube is that more of the water reaches the end of the hose, and faster. The result of a strong myelin sheath along a neural pathway is that more of the signals triggered by your thinking reach their destinations stronger and faster.

The results of neuron memory are obvious to see in athletes who can repeat an action over and over again reliably. Stephen Curry of the NBA swishes 3 pointer after 3 pointer (especially in practice sessions). Tom Brady of the NFL hits receivers in stride year after year. Curt Schilling of MLB throws 100 MPH strikes, and Simone Biles of the USA Olympics team does more flips off the vault than I can count in the time it takes her to do them. They have neuron memory and can repeat those actions precisely because they have so many neural connections that have built up a thick protection of myelin sheaths to make sure the signals quickly and reliably reach their destination.

While not as obvious, similar neuron connections are created for mental tasks as well, which is why great chess grandmasters like Magnus Carlsen can see and process a chessboard so much more quickly than you or me. They've seen the pieces in similar orientations already and can chunk (grab the position as a whole) and then process the information quickly. Instead of having to look at each piece, they can analyze the position as a whole, and where the likely next moves will be, based on different available move possibilities. A computer has to analyze each move and follow it through with all the possible permutations. The computer can succeed using the iterative process because it can make all the individual computations incredibly fast. Mathematicians, scientists, or any expert in their respective fields also have a wealth of knowledge built up by years of practice that allow them to quickly access and process related information quickly.

Learning also applies to interpersonal relationships. We learn how to react to people starting at birth, and those reactions are practiced. The more we practice them, the easier they become to repeat.

We learn to be excited when we're going to see our grandparents. Then we get excited faster the second and third times we're on our way to see them. When we dread seeing the bully at school, it's easier and faster to experience that dread when we see the next encounter coming. When you are annoyed at someone's bad habit - the more you see it and the more you get annoyed, the faster and more reliably you get annoyed the next time. We have an adage: "They argue like an old married couple." That old married couple has learned how to get upset at each other, and if they have things that bug them, they can easily go from perfectly happy to upset from a triggering activity nearly instantly. In this case, it's the neural connections that trigger the amygdala that controls fear and anger. It's all learned and ingrained because of strong neural connections that have built up myelin sheaths, or what society calls something that comes easily after many repetitions: "muscle memory". The upsetting trigger could be something as innocuous as a dirty sock left on the floor by a spouse. The first time it happens, it's not a big deal. It just takes a second to pick it up and rectify the situation. When it's the 100th time it happens, a swift and heated emotional reaction can result. It's still a single dirty sock on the floor, but the emotional response has been learned and the neural memory makes sure all the signal gets to where it's going, and fast.

Similar reactions can happen between people groups. If you're taught (directly or indirectly) to avoid, fear, or despise a different people group and that fear is reinforced, those feelings and reactions will surface more and more quickly and reliably as those neuron connections grow and the myelin sheaths protect the signals. The reactions could be triggered by something as innocent as meeting your friendly school district rival or sports team, or as sinister as encountering a competing violent gang.

Don't be discouraged if you recognize a negative reaction you have to a person, an annoying habit, or even a people group. You can change your reaction. You can rewire your brain. If you learn to recognize your negative reaction and deliberately choose to have a different reaction, you can learn how to react differently. It will take time and effort to let the old neural connections and their myelin sheaths atrophy, but the less you use them, the weaker those connections will become. The more you use your new reaction, the stronger those connections will become.

The brain is malleable. It can change. It can learn and grow and even unlearn with time, patience, and practice.

I practiced juggling 3 balls so much that I had phenomenal "muscle memory." The neural connections that controlled throwing balls from one hand to the other were strong, and the myelin sheaths that protected those signals were thick. I already held the Guinness World Records title for the longest duration blindfolded juggling. How much longer could I juggle blindfolded?

I coordinated the attempt with the event organizers a few weeks out and started practicing. Sometimes I would need to run to warm up my body before starting to blindfold juggle since 3 ball juggling doesn't get my blood flowing or heart rate up. Sometimes I would start blindfolded juggling without warming up which led to more muscle fatigue since my blood flow was insufficient to feed the few muscles that were working. In practice, I quickly matched my previous Guinness World Records-mark and regularly surpassed it. My goal was to juggle at least 15 minutes without the use of my eyes, but hopefully longer. I practiced at lunch and usually made a couple runs of a few minutes and sometimes longer. My longest blindfolded juggling run (and personal record to this day) was one day at lunch after practicing for slow juggling. I stood on the tennis courts of Boise High School and had a particularly long run. It was past time to end my lunch and get back to the office, so I stopped juggling without dropping a ball. I looked at my watch and discovered I had been blind juggling for 29 minutes. Would I be able to match that mark when it counted?

On the day of the attempt, I got warmed up by juggling and running to burn off the extra adrenaline in my system. Since I had gone on the TODAY show and had the nervous adrenaline spike, my body was more susceptible to repeating that reaction. I told the witnesses that I was going to attempt the record multiple times, which helped take the pressure off and made it more likely that I wouldn't have a nervous reaction.

On the day of the attempt at the Cradlepoint party, there were two local news stations with cameras rolling which added to the pressure. I started the first run and juggled a few minutes before dropping a ball. I tried again but soon dropped a ball. And then did again and again. I got close to 6 minutes but dropped a ball before I broke the record. I kept getting nervous when I got close to breaking my previous Guinness World Records title. My body produced too much adrenaline, and I'd get shaky and drop a ball. I was conflicted about what I did next, but I finally decided to grab a beer and drink some to help myself relax. I think it may have helped since just a little alcohol produces a calming effect. I also tried with and without noise-canceling headphones to see if that made a difference. I theorized that I might be more focused if I blocked out the noise. The inner ear, however, is critical for balance and when my eyes are shut, the inner ear becomes even more important for balance since I have no visual references. In the end, I decided not to use the headphones because I felt disoriented with them since my inner ear was confused. Finally, I got a run of more than 7 minutes passing my previous Guinness World Records-mark before I dropped a ball. I was happy and celebrated, but I was not thrilled. I did interviews for the news stations, and then they left. The pressure was now off, and I decided to go for one last run. This one went well. I juggled blindfolded for 22 minutes 7 seconds before I finally dropped a ball and the attempt ended. I was simultaneously excited and disappointed. I more than tripled the previous record, but it felt like there was no reason why I shouldn't have been able to keep going for hours. Maybe someday I will. In the meantime, there are many other skills - both physical as well as mental - that I would like to learn or replace with new learnings. And I know I can change because my brain is plastic, malleable, and extraordinarily adaptive. Yours is too. How would you like to change it? Now that you know it's possible, I challenge you to try.

Longest Duration Blindfolded Juggling (3 Balls)
Previous Record: 6 minutes 34 seconds (held by me)
New Record: 22 minutes 7 seconds

15
DEVELOPING GRIT

Fewest Juggling Catches in One Minute (3 Balls)
Previous Record: 30 catches

In the second chapter, I illustrated how grit, as described by Angela Duckworth, is a better predictor of success than talent, genius, or natural ability. That's interesting, but it's about as useful as saying having money is the easiest way to buy all the stuff you want. What's more useful is knowing how to get the money. Or in this case, how can I become gritty? Or is grit even something that can be developed? Like the answer to how to become a millionaire, it isn't as simple as an arithmetic problem: work for 10,000 hours while getting paid $100/hour and you'll be a millionaire.

Grit is intangible. It's not something that can be easily measured, but several markers can be observed, and there is evidence to suggest that grit can be developed. Grit can be defined as working hard toward a goal for a prolonged period even when, or especially when, obstacles get in your way. Grit isn't just working with passion; it's working with passion for a long time. It's not just about making progress toward a goal; it's about not giving up when progress isn't being made. If you keep hitting the same wall that stops progress, it's usually best to get help, try another approach, or take a brief pause before trying again, but don't give up.

One of the best ways to develop grit is to act like you have it. What I mean by that is you should do things that make you look gritty: don't give up, stick with your goals, and when you want to take a day off, don't. If you practice the disciplines that make you look gritty, you develop grit. When you're getting started and haven't built up the willpower, the discipline, and the habits that make you gritty, you may find you slip up. When pursuing a goal, you may miss a day, not do the extra lap, eat too much, sleep in, or otherwise take a step back. DO NOT USE THIS AS AN EXCUSE TO GIVE UP! Just because you missed one activity doesn't mean you have failed. People too often use a single failure as an excuse to give up and miss all the rest of the days too. Look at New Year's resolutions. Some studies show that the average New Year's resolution lasts only a few days. It's hard to stick with a new goal, especially when you're not used to sticking with a goal. People use the first miss to throw in the towel. I didn't make it that day, so I guess I'm off the hook now. Was the goal worth pursuing or not? If so, keep pursuing it.

Having grit, however, doesn't mean you can't give up at all. Sometimes you need to move on to another goal, or you've decided the goal you set isn't one you, or your team, or your company should keep pursuing. You shouldn't give up when it's easiest to give up (like when you first hit a challenge). If you're going to give up, give up at a natural end. It could be at the end of a pilot project or program checkpoint. For an athlete, it would be at the end of a sports season (not in the middle of a grueling stairs workout halfway through the season). If you're going to quit, it should be a conscious choice when you're "out of the frying pan" and don't feel overwhelmed anymore. You're also not allowed to give up regularly. You need to see passions and goals through for many years to develop grit. If you're hopping from one project to the next, even with great passion and vigor at the outset, but not sticking with them long term through challenges and setbacks, you're not developing grit.

When colleges are evaluating applicants, they're not looking for students who have tried two dozen different activities but didn't stick with any (However, I don't discourage trying a lot of activities; it helps you discover what you like and don't like). They're looking for students who stick with a few activities long term and make progress. For example, in sports, they look for progression: like joining a team as a freshman, making the junior varsity squad as a sophomore, starting on the varsity squad as a junior, and making captain as a senior. In a club setting, joining as a freshman, lettering as a sophomore, taking on leadership as a junior, and completing a keystone project as a senior. If a college sees an applicant who tried 15 different activities but didn't stick with at least 2 or 3 of them long term, it's now considered a red flag.

The United States Military Academy at West Point now knows that grit is the number one indicator of long-term success, more so than academic achievement, strength, stamina, money, race, socio-economic background, pedigree, recommendations, or any other measurable factor. West Point looks for applicants who have grit.

When you're developing grit, Angela Duckworth recommends picking a hard thing and sticking with it for at least two years. It becomes your hard thing. A hard thing is a goal, passion, or hobby you want to work on to improve. It needs to be challenging, have milestones you can reach, and require regular effort and deliberate practice to get better. I have chosen several hard things to work on in the past few years, and one was the goal of becoming the world's slowest juggler. The record is defined as the fewest juggling catches in one minute. The time starts when the juggling begins, and the attempt is disqualified if a ball is dropped or two balls are caught in the same hand before the minute is over.

I find it ironic that to become the slowest juggler in the world, I had to throw the juggling balls the fastest.

Slow juggling requires throwing the balls to a great height, which means not only throwing them up with as much velocity as possible but also catching them when they're coming down at their maximum velocity. There is another subtle aspect to slow juggling that makes it difficult to master. To minimize the number of catches in one minute, not only do you have to maximize the height and hang time of each throw, you need to minimize the hang time overlap of each throw. This means as one ball is coming down, you must wait until the last possible moment to throw the next ball up. The vertical velocity of my well-thrown ball is about 35 miles per hour going up. This means that when I catch it at the same height from which I threw, it is also moving down at 35 miles per hour due to the conservation of energy (with some speed loss due to air drag). I wait until the last possible moment to throw the next ball up at 35 miles per hour and immediately have to catch the ball coming down if I've timed it right. This means the speed differential between my hand and the falling ball is nearly 70 miles per hour an instant before the catch. To make the catch, that speed difference needs to get to zero quickly. More than a few times in practice my hands took a nasty blow when I mistimed the catch and had to absorb the full impact. Sometimes it felt like my hand got hit by a 70-mile-per-hour baseball pitch and hurt so badly I had to take the rest of the day off as well as the next to let the bruising heal.

Before I could face such a painful dilemma, I first had to consistently throw the balls exactly vertically. This was harder at first than it may seem. Many people have significant practice throwing balls primarily horizontally in an arc from football, baseball, basketball, or myriad other ball sports. Few people have any reason to regularly attempt to throw a ball straight up, and even less, as hard as they can. For those who have tried, some things become readily obvious. The harder you throw it, the harder it is to be accurate and the more any error is amplified. It was not an uncommon occurrence for me to throw a ball up from the middle of a tennis court and watch it fall over 50 feet from me on the other side of the fence lining the court. Even the best throws usually required at least a step or two to get into position for the catch.

There was no official Guinness World Record-mark for this record when I decided I wanted to break it. The juggling community and JuggleWikia tracks this record, and the best mark was 30 catches. Guinness World Records approved my application and used 30 catches as the maximum mark to qualify as a Guinness World Records title. This meant each throw needed to average more than two seconds of hangtime. Thirty catches times two seconds of hangtime per throw equals one minute. Plus, there are two balls in the air right before each catch with both their hangtime clocks ticking, which is why the average hang time must be slightly over two seconds.

I started practicing. At first, I practiced in my driveway, and then I realized I needed more space and moved to the cul-de-sac across the street from my house. Each practice session required a few minutes to warm up, and then I was able to get on pace for less than 30 catches in a minute. I didn't often finish a full minute run, but I was confident I would be able to break the record.

I then found an older juggling video that was recently posted to JuggleWikia. The video showed a professional juggler slow juggling in a gym. He got 26 catches in one minute. It wasn't validated by Guinness World Records, but I didn't want to have a hollow victory by breaking a Guinness World Records title while not breaking the overall world record (like with the 5-ball speed juggling record). My new target to beat was 26 catches, meaning I was shooting for 25 or less. I practiced for months.

The sharp upward throwing motion made the triceps muscles below my upper arm so sore I could barely move them the day after an intense practice session. If I took more than a couple of days off from practice, the feeling in my arms after a practice session was like that of the day after doing lifting squats when you haven't in a long time - intensely sore.

Eventually, I was able to complete a couple of full minute runs with only 25 catches in practice, but I knew I could do better. I could throw the balls higher, just not consistently. I filmed my practice and reviewed the video to put the throw and catch time of every ball during a minute into an excel spreadsheet to measure the hangtime. After doing some number crunching, I discovered that if every throw was the best I had during that minute, I could theoretically get down to 21 catches in a minute. The best I thought I could do in real life was 23. Even after months of practice, I would only get 23 catches once every few hours across several practice sessions, but 23 was now my new goal. And then winter hit in Boise. It was so cold and snowy I couldn't practice outside anymore, and I had no access to buildings with 40-foot ceilings which is much higher than a typical gym ceiling. I took some time off to practice and break a few other records. By November before the next winter, I was almost ready.

Practice like you have grit already and you can develop grit.

I lifted weights, timed every slow juggling run, and counted every catch. I went outside to practice even when I didn't want to or when I could have found an excuse like the weather threatening rain. I filmed my practice sessions to identify tendencies and weaknesses and analyzed my throws with data.

I had to determine which balls would be best to use. Would I want larger ones that were easier to see, round ones that were easier to throw, or smaller ones that I could throw higher and were less likely to collide with other balls? I settled on the smaller "Gballz n8's" that are small and underfilled but have a dense plastic resin and metal beads for added weight. I could get a more consistent high throw with them when I snapped my arm up with a forceful motion while jumping up than with any other ball. They were harder to see since they were small, but they were also less likely to collide.

After months of practice, I was ready to break the record. I decided the blue turf at Boise State University would provide the perfect backdrop with a recognizable location and plenty of open space to run around without having to look where I was going. I contacted the athletics department and they were gracious enough to let me and a team of witnesses, photographers, timers, and videographers have access to the field for an hour.

It was a cold November day with temperatures in the 30°Fs when I showed up at Albertsons Stadium. I was a little worried about the Guinness World Records team getting cold, but I knew I would be fine. This was the most physically exhausting record I had attempted to date, and I wasn't worried about staying warm once I got moving. I would regularly measure my heart rate at the end of a one-minute run and find it pounding over 170 beats per minute. My resting heart rate after 2,000 miles running and juggling was only about 50 beats per minute.

The witnesses, timers, photographer, and videographers all met me outside the stadium, and we were escorted in by our contact. I had four video cameras set up to make sure I would always be in at least one frame. During an attempt, I ran around so much that I often left the frame of one or two cameras in practice, so I decided to play it safe. Even though I had warmed up outside the stadium, I still needed more to reach my peak. The physical exertion and warmup cycle are like that of a baseball pitcher, and the maximum throwing speed doesn't come quickly.

The clock starts as soon as I make the first throw, and I needed to juggle for a full minute without a drop to break the record. On the first attempt, I dropped a ball before the minute was up, and again on the second, and the third attempts. On the fourth attempt, I finished the minute with 24 catches. I raised my arms in the air and ran to the camera to document the accomplishment. But I wasn't satisfied. I knew I could throw higher. I was completely warmed up now, so I threw higher. This time it took me 11 more attempts before I finished a full minute. I was throwing higher, so each little mistake was magnified even more. Little mistakes became catastrophic. But on the 15th overall try, time was called after only 23 catches. I was stoked. I was still feeling good, and it had taken less than 15 minutes for all the tries, so I asked the team to stick around for a little longer to see if I could get even less.

When I started again, I threw each ball with as much snapping upward force as my arms and legs could muster. I wasn't just warmed up; I was hot and in the zone. At the end of a particularly close fail where I almost completed the minute, I collapsed to the ground. The effort was exhausting. I loved it. I was so close, but I needed a break.

On my 21st try, I threw the balls over 45 feet into the air. The field goal posts nearby at the end of the football field were only 30 feet high for reference. Every time I threw a ball, I jumped. My legs left the ground with my hand outstretched high above my head and about eight feet above the blue field. The oncoming ball came down with a 70-mile-per-hour speed differential relative to my hand, and I had to quickly lower my hand to soften the blow. I watched the upward flying ball to determine where it would land. I then quickly shuffled under it with several small steps like tennis players do to ensure they are in the perfect position to hit the ball with power. If I were off the center of the four cameras' focus, I deliberately threw the next ball back toward the center so I could stay in the frame. On my last run, every throw was nearly perfect. My arms were taut like rubber bands and when the 23rd throw reached its apex and would be well over a second before it came back down to be caught, time was called. I had broken the record with my personal best of only 22 completed catches in one minute. I yelled "Come On!" to celebrate and ran toward the main camera to capture my excitement on film. I announced my 22-catch victory between gasping breaths trying to recover from the physical exertion. It took several minutes before my rapidly beating heart slowed since it was beating over three times its resting rate.

I was now the slowest juggler in the world. I beat the previous official record by nearly 30% and the best-known run ever by nearly 20%. I calculated that it's physically possible for me to achieve 21 catches in one minute. It would take my best throw of the record-breaking run for every throw. I could also get 20 catches in one minute if I got just a little bit better and had perfect throws. I'll save that challenge for another time.

I picked slow juggling as my hard thing. I stuck with it for a season. I worked hard with deliberate practice regularly. I timed every run, counted every catch, and tracked my progress. I didn't give up until I completed my goal - even when that goal was extended and pushed as I set my sights higher and higher. But for now, I've given it up. I didn't quit until there was a natural end. Other naturals ends could be the end of a sports season, the end of a school course, or the end of a work project. I no longer regularly practice slow juggling since I've moved on to other things, but if this record is challenged, I will likely return. For now, I will enjoy the accomplishment.

Fewest Juggling Catches in one Minute (3 Balls)

Previous Record: 30 catches (Guinness World Records),
26 catches (Juggling community w/video evidence)
New Record: 22 catches

16
WHEN EASY ISN'T EASY

Fewest Juggling Catches in One Minute (4 Balls)
Previous Record: 74 catches

Part of grit is picking your hard thing and sticking with it. If you quit when things get hard, or even after they've been hard for a long time, you're not developing grit. You can quit, but not when you're feeling down or in the most difficult stage of a challenge. That's the easy road out, and it doesn't build grit. If you quit on a down day, it feels like failure. Instead, push through the challenge on a hard day and find a natural breaking point before you reevaluate whether to continue or not. You can avoid failure and avoid giving up by making a conscious decision to move on while not under duress. You can make a rational decision to set aside whatever you've been doing and avoid the feeling of failure that comes along with quitting when things get hard.

After a year of training to break the record for the world's slowest juggling, I decided to quit. I quit after achieving my goal; it was a natural end. But I also saw an opportunity. I had spent so much time building up the muscles, visual acuity, and skillset needed for slow juggling that I decided to leverage that effort. There is another juggling record for fewest juggling catches in one minute with four balls. It's not tracked by Guinness World Records, but it is by the juggling community on JuggleWikia. It appeared relatively achievable compared to the three-ball slow juggling record I had just shattered. The throws didn't need to go nearly as high, but about three times as many throws would be required (with three times the opportunities to make an error). Each throw isn't as high and there are at least two balls in the air at any given moment, so there are about three to four times as many throws and catches in one minute compared to three-ball slow juggling.

I decided before I put slow juggling on the shelf as my hard thing for a season that I should break the four-ball slow juggling record first. I could leverage the skills I'd developed and get one qualifying four-ball juggling run on camera to break this unofficial world record. It ended up being much harder than I expected.

When I juggle three balls, I throw one ball up just before the falling ball lands and immediately catch the oncoming ball. I then have a few seconds to position myself under the next falling ball. When juggling four balls, the standard pattern is to juggle two balls in each hand independently. This means there are always at least two balls in the air. When I throw a ball there is already one at the apex of its arc about to come down to the other hand. I also have less than half the time to get into position to catch the next ball. This means that any error in a throw is even harder to recover from. When I throw one ball a little too far forward and then the next one a little behind, I have to move forward toward the ball I need to catch next while simultaneously moving farther away from the one thrown backward I need to catch after that. To stabilize my movement, I have to throw the next ball up and behind me. It will then land closer to the ball which is already in the air.

I set up a camera to catch my attempts on video. I stood outside in the middle of the cul-de-sac flailing my arms in the air and jumping every second while I chased balls back and forth across the pavement like an excited puppy being tormented by a kid with a laser pointer. I had a blast. My wife didn't want to come outside for fear the neighbors might see her while I looked the fool.

I planned to set up a camera on a Saturday, get one qualifying one-minute run in without a drop and put the slow juggling hard thing on the shelf. Getting it on camera was key, as otherwise, it would not count, even for the unofficial record. Guinness World Records is much stricter and has several more requirements for evidence collection and verification, but for the unofficial record, I just needed to stay in the frame. I would restart the camera every few attempts, so the files wouldn't get too large. After an hour of four-ball slow juggling on Saturday morning, I had to take a break. I was exhausted. I would juggle well for part of a minute, but then one bad throw would make it all fall apart. The initial error was compounded by the other ball in the air landing in a different spot than the bad throw. Every errant throw would require two corrections before the juggling pattern would stabilize again.

On Saturday afternoon, I went out again for over an hour to make another attempt at the record. I didn't concede defeat for the day until it was too dark to see the balls. I wasn't giving up, but I realized this wasn't going to be as easy as setting up a camera and breaking the record at will. No matter how weak and easily achievable I initially thought the record was, it was still hard.

On Sunday I tried again. I tossed balls in the air until I was drenched in sweat. My arms ached from the effort. I was so close to finishing a full minute, I could taste it. For dozens of attempts, I was on pace for far less than 60 catches. To increase the chances of finishing a full minute, I experimented with not throwing as hard to see if I could reduce the number of errant throws. It required more throws, but each was easier to execute. After several unsuccessful attempts at lower throw speeds, I would ratchet back up the toss height and see how far into the minute I could make it. It required fewer throws but was harder to execute. I got dozens of runs over 30 seconds, several over 45, and a two over 50 seconds. I only needed to avoid dropping a ball for a few more seconds to break the record. I alternated between throwing up as hard as I could, under throwing, and medium strength throws.

After hours of effort, on one of the juggling runs with lower tosses, I finally finished the full minute. I achieved 68 catches. It was far more than I thought I should be able to get but still good enough to break the record. I was elated. It wasn't until a few seconds after I finished the minute that I panicked. I had spent all day turning the video recording on and off to keep the files small, and I wasn't sure I had started the recording before the last run. I had started and stopped it so many times, I wasn't sure if it was running or not. Without video evidence, my effort would have been nothing but personal validation that I could do it. Even an unofficial record listing requires video evidence.

Fortunately, the video footage was there.

I posted it on YouTube. I had worked for months to become the slowest juggler in the world, and then I decided to tack on an unofficial record. I thought it would be easy, but it still took two full days and a significant amount of effort. It was now time to put this hard thing - slow juggling - on the shelf. I would still work on developing grit, acting gritty, and sticking with what I started, but different projects were calling my name now that I had set the world record for slow juggling with both three and four balls. I didn't give up at the start, or when it got hard. I even extended my original goal of setting the three-ball record by shattering it and then breaking the four-ball record too. The biggest surprise was that even though I was the best in the world at slow juggling three balls, slow juggling four was still a significant challenge. I expected it to be easy, but it wasn't. Sometimes we're disappointed when we don't do as well at something as we expect. This isn't a reflection of our potential or proof that we were never good at the activity. Sometimes, perseverance is required even when we think it shouldn't be. Keep working to persevere and any interim challenges or failures will end with eventual success.

Fewest Juggling Catches in One Minute (4 Balls)
Previous Record: 74 catches
New Record: 68 catches

17
SUPERPOWERS

Fastest 10 Meters with a Cue Balanced on the Chin
Previous Record 3.02 seconds

In *Moonwalking with Einstein*, Joshua Foer follows the American Memory Championships. These are somewhat obscure competitions where people compete in feats of memory. The competition includes tasks such as quickly memorizing the order of a shuffled deck of cards. People compete in random number memorization. They memorize names assigned to random faces. They memorize and recite digits of pi and not just the first 50 digits I had memorized since celebrating Pi Day in high school; some of them memorize thousands or tens of thousands of digits of pi.

The most shocking thing to me isn't that these people can perform these feats, though it is extraordinary. The most shocking thing is that when the competitors are asked when they realized they had such an extraordinary memory, most simply say that they don't.

How is this possible? It seems incredulous that an average person could learn to be able to memorize a random deck of cards in less than 5 minutes (or for those most practiced, in under 30 seconds). Can anyone memorize random lists of hundreds of items at will? The answer is simple - yes, with practice. The "memory champions," or so they're called, learn tricks and tools that allow them to more effectively encode information, so the human brain remembers and recalls it quickly. Then they practice for hours, and days, and months on end. It may seem like being able to remember virtually anything would be a covetable skill, but it's not necessarily practical. Most of us have externalized much of our memory. We use our devices, calendars, notes, and cell phones to record information, so we don't have to expend effort remembering it. We even use other people to remember things for us, especially in the case of spouses. If you're married, think about the times you've asked your spouse someone's name multiple times or where something is, knowing they'll remember it, but you never do. Our cell phones give reminders, shopping lists are written down, calendars keep our schedule, and spouses remember our nephews' and nieces' birthdays. We could all learn these memory techniques to remember all of that information. The catch is that the effort and practice required to learn these techniques is extensive, so it probably wouldn't save you time.

Joshua Foer was skeptical of the claim that a person with an average memory could learn and perform such amazing memory feats until he decided to try it himself. He started as an average guy with an average memory and studied with memory champions for a year. He learned the tricks of the trade and practiced relentlessly. He practiced regularly, and he practiced deliberately. A year later, you know what happened to this average guy? He won the American Memory Championships.

We see those with abilities far beyond ours and assume they must be special. It's a lot easier and feels safer to say that the amazing skill we're witnessing is unattainable for us than it is to admit it is our failure to try that prevents us from being able to do those same things. We can't dedicate ourselves to mastering every skill, there simply isn't enough time in life. But you shouldn't let yourself view others as endowed with skills unattainable by yourself and use that as an excuse to never try. I believe we should all pick several skills to master in life. When you need to learn a new skill, don't let prejudices get in the way of trying by saying that it takes an inborn natural talent you don't have. If you put in the hard work, you can get it done. You can learn to do anything you want to if you put in enough time, energy, and effort.

I read about the Guinness World Records title for the fastest 10 meters on foot balancing a pool cue on the chin. Instead of thinking the person who set the record had some special skill I couldn't attain, I decided I would practice breaking it myself. It helped that I already had the fundamental skill of balancing things on my face, which in itself is a skill most anyone can learn with time and effort.

I got my pool cue and first decided to see how fast I could walk 10 meters with it balanced on my chin. I walked slowly on the first attempt and then sped up my pace on subsequent tries. After a few practices, my fast walking speed was nowhere near the 3.02-second record mark. I was taking close to 10 seconds to cover 10 meters. I was going to have to run.

I found an open space to practice on the ground floor of Cradlepoint's lobby. The company I work for shares a building with other tenants, but I figured that a corner of the lobby was all right to use temporarily. I blocked off a section with chairs and a line of juggling balls on the floor to create a perimeter. I wanted to divert the foot traffic away from my 10-meter sprint lane. I stared up toward the sky for each practice and could neither see where I was going nor what I might hit. I carefully scoped out the area and any foot traffic just before putting the cue on my chin and aborted the attempt if I didn't start immediately. I looked around to determine if there were any risks, put the cue on my chin, and took off.

There are two particularly challenging parts of this record attempt. When moving at a constant velocity, especially when the velocity is zero, it isn't particularly difficult to keep the cue balanced on my chin. The hard parts are one, accelerating, and two, running straight. I had to not only travel 10 meters, but the rules also required the attempt to take place within a track lane. Stepping out of the lane disqualifies the attempt.

When I accelerate forward with a cue balanced upright on my chin, the bottom of the cue comes with me since it's in contact with my chin, but the top stays in place due to inertia and the cue falls back relative to me. This means I have to let the cue fall forward before I begin accelerating forward. It falls slowly at first, so before I start moving, I have to move my chin sharply backward to start it falling forward. I then have to accelerate forward at the same rate the cue is falling forward. If I accelerate too slowly, the cue continues to fall forward and off my chin. If I accelerate too quickly, the cue stands back up straight and I cannot accelerate further without it falling off backward. Finding the perfect cue falling rate to equal my maximum acceleration was the trickiest part to master.

The second challenge was staying in my lane. Running straight for 10 meters without being able to see the ground is tricky enough. Looking straight up makes it harder since it throws off my sense of balance. Doing it while a cue is tipping not only forward and back but also sideways makes this a consummate challenge.

I first had to ensure the cue started falling straight forward and then had to keep it from drifting sideways as I ran. My neck and chin would often jut out to the side, trying to get a drifting cue back to the center. I regularly made 10-meter runs thinking I did well only to discover I had left the lane 9 meters into the run.

I practiced at lunch during work. I didn't have ready access to many indoor locations with 15 meters of open space (including 1 meter to stand at the start and 4 meters to stop), and tall ceilings and so, unlike many of my practices, this one was visible to lots of people seeing my every failure right from the start. They were people I knew and worked with regularly. Our lobby is also viewable from all the upper floors with a giant central skylight that shines down from the roof, and I heard about several groups watching from above trying to figure out what on earth I was doing.

I scheduled the attempt at the Boise State University Science and Engineering Festival. It was exactly one year after setting my second Guinness World Records title at the same event. I prepared a half-hour talk and planned to finish with this record attempt.

Before the talk, the witnesses and I measured out and marked off a 10-meter-long lane with masking tape following the width requirements set forth by the international track and field governing bodies. I took several practices with my practice cue and just a couple with my official cue that met the Guinness World Records regulations. I had dropped my practice cue several times and broken and glued it back together on multiple occasions. I didn't want to risk breaking my official cue with no time to fix it.

A couple of hundred students and their families attended the talk promoting STEM education. The Guinness World Records title attempt was my final act. I explained the rules to the audience, what I was doing, and the current record. I then put the cue on my chin and waited for the "ready, set, go!" from my timers. I was off. I had a slight stutter step at the beginning but still ran through the end without a drop. It was too easy. At least it looked too easy. I was told by several people after the fact that I needed to fail a couple of times to build the suspense. Or I should have had someone else try to balance the cue on their chin to show just how hard it was. Instead, there were 2.51 seconds of near-flawless execution.

It didn't look difficult to my audience.

Most people have some experience trying to memorize lists of information and numbers and 'know' they can't do it. Placing a cue on their chin and running 10 meters is not quite as obvious - especially if it doesn't look hard. The naivety about how difficult something is supposed to be can work in your favor.

I love that about how kids learn. They don't know they're not supposed to be able to do something until they're told. Learning how to walk is an exceedingly difficult activity, and yet most master it. If we put as much effort into learning other tasks as we did in learning how to walk, we could learn to do nearly anything.

I recognize that running 10 meters with a cue balanced on the chin is not a particularly useful skill or one I would recommend anyone else practice. But never say you can't do something just because you haven't put in the effort. You can certainly appreciate the effort others have put in to master their craft, which is why we watch sports and love the Olympics. By saying you could never do what someone else has done simply creates a self-fulfilling prophecy instead of leaving the door open to a new adventure.

Fastest 10 Meters Balancing a Pool Cue on a Chin
Previous Record: 3.02 seconds
New Record: 2.51 seconds

18

FIND A PURPOSE, EVEN WHEN ONE ISN'T OBVIOUS

Furthest Distance Walked Balancing a Lawnmower on the Chin
Previous Record: 122 meters

When I told people I was planning to walk over 100 meters with a lawnmower on my chin, the response was never "Why?" but rather "Will it be running?" I suppose that is a natural enough question, and I do hope to someday break the record for distance walked with a running lawnmower on my chin, but this particular record's rules specified that a non-powered lawnmower must be used.

"Why?" is the better question. The answer is the same as to why I break any record: to promote STEM education; challenge and better myself; and to show that if you set your mind to a goal, believe in yourself, and pursue it with a passion, you can accomplish virtually anything.

I decided I would attempt to walk further with a lawnmower balanced on my chin than anyone ever had before. This is easier said than done.

Finding a suitable lawnmower was the other thing that took the longest to prepare for this record. The minimum weight set by Guinness World Records is only 7 kg or just over 15 lbs. Most lawnmowers are much heavier, often 60 or more pounds for a push mower and 500 pounds for a riding mower (ok, so I never actually considered using a riding lawnmower). Push-powered mowers (with no engine) are mostly metal and usually weigh 30-60 pounds, while gasoline-powered mowers start at 60 pounds and only go up. I didn't want to make this attempt too much harder on myself than necessary. No structural modifications are allowed either, so you can't find one and strip off the extra weight. After months of looking, I finally found one in the back corner of a thrift store that was the lightest one I'd ever picked up. Even though I didn't have a scale with me to confirm the weight, I was confident it was light enough I could make an attempt with it. It was a used push-powered lawnmower with dead grass clippings still clinging to the metal blades that had long lost their polish. In other words, it was perfect. I gave the thrift store $20 and took it home.

When I got it home, I discovered it was 23 pounds. While 8 pounds heavier than necessary, or 50% over the required minimum weight, the lawnmower had a padded handle to protect my chin. The muscles in the back of my neck hurt the most during a long heavyweight chin balance. It creates a sharp burning pain similar to what you might feel in your abs while holding a plank for a long time. My lower back is what hurts the next day if I overdo it, and permanent damage to my spine is my biggest concern. I usually balance objects on my chin while stationary, so learning to balance while walking presented a few challenges.

The first challenge was the extra movement. The movement of my body throws off the center of gravity of the lawnmower and requires extra adjustments to keep it directly above my chin. With lighter objects, I can simply move my neck forward, back, or to either side to bring the point of contact on my face directly under the center of gravity of the object. With a 23-pound lawnmower torquing down on my neck, that's not an option. I must bring my entire body under the center of gravity since my neck needs to be lined up with my spine to support that much weight.

The second challenge is walking in the right direction. When I have the lawnmower on my chin, I must look straight up at it to keep it balanced. I can usually take a few steps in the right direction, but after making several minor balancing corrections moving side to side, my internal gyroscope starts drifting. To walk more than about 10 meters, I need more references than my internal gyroscope. The best solution to this problem is a reference point I can see out of the corner of my eye while staring up. A power line, trees, or a building off to the side work well. While walking around a track there are usually no consistent reference points visible. When there is a reference point visible, I'm not always sure where it is relative to the track and myself.

Another trick I used is following verbal instructions from another person. When I start walking off track, a person says I need to move left or right. This is okay, but I found it was not precise enough. The most helpful strategy was to be told what lane I'm in and when I cross into another lane. I start in lane two and have someone tell me whenever I crossed over into another lane. If I went into lane one, I would immediately correct back into lane two so as not to risk leaving the track. As soon as I crossed back into lane two, I would be told I was back in lane two. If I crossed into lane three, I would correct back into lane two. I was more careful to avoid crossing inside of lane one since leaving the track could void an attempt as the distance couldn't be guaranteed, and I might trip on uneven ground with a lawnmower balanced on my chin. If I went into lanes four or five, I might end up walking further than required, but at least I could still claim the distance walked around the track (and not trip on uneven ground).

Another challenge I often found looking up in the sky was the sun. I tried to avoid this one for obvious reasons. When it's behind the lawnmower in my line-of-sight, I can't keep my eyes open. No matter how hard I tried, even with sunglasses, I couldn't keep my eyes open for more than a few seconds with the sun in my field of vision, and the lawnmower would always fall off my chin. I made sure to practice at the track the same time of day as I was going to break the record to simulate the conditions and ensure the sun would not be an issue.

I contacted Aaron, the Boise High School track coach, and asked if I could give a short talk and set a record for the team. He graciously obliged.

I showed up at the track a few minutes early to meet with the Guinness World Records verification team, weigh the lawnmower, warm up, and prep for the record attempt. After giving a short talk, I had the track team accompany me halfway around the track 200 meters away. I recruited two students to hold crepe paper across the finish line. I had another student operate a stationary camera near the finish on the bleachers, and a fourth held a GoPro in his hands while walking backward in front of me to film the entire attempt close-up.

I lined up at the 200-meter start line, placed the lawnmower on my chin, and started walking. I had Mike, a coworker, gently call out the lanes to keep me on the track. The verbal instructions were most helpful while rounding the first 100-meter turn but still critical on the 100-meter straightaway. An unexpected fear that cropped up during the official record attempt was caused by the students walking with me. I told them they could walk along with me, but I didn't give them any instructions about how far away to walk. I couldn't tell how close they were, but with all the talking and excitement, it felt like they were less than the length of a falling lawnmower away. I walked slowly to make sure I didn't drop the lawnmower, and it took me longer than expected to finish the 200 meters. The mark to beat was 122 meters but I didn't want to go through the trouble of measuring the exact distance manually, so I wanted to cross the 200-meter finish line. It took me 3 minutes 40 seconds traveling at about a 30-minute mile pace. I was expecting it to take less than 3 minutes, but with the adrenaline running through my body, it felt shorter while taking longer.

Only later when I watched the video did I see that the lead cameraperson had to duck under the finish line to avoid breaking the crepe paper stretched across it as we approached. I'm glad he was paying attention. I didn't see the crepe paper, but when I hit it, I felt it on my belly. I took one additional step to ensure I had passed the 200-meter mark and then removed the lawnmower from my chin. I then raised it above my head in celebration, enjoyed the excitement of the Boise High School track team, and hoped the message that they can accomplish anything they set their mind to was just as exciting because that was my purpose.

Furthest Distance Walked Balancing a Lawnmower on the Chin
Previous Record: 122 meters
New Record: 200 meters

19
POWERING THROUGH

Longest Duration Balancing a Lawnmower on the Chin
Previous Record: 5 minutes 1 second

Just a few days after setting the Guinness World Records title for greatest distance walked balancing a lawnmower on the chin, I had the opportunity to set the record for the longest duration balancing a lawnmower on the chin. I had it scheduled before I made the walking attempt but ran into a problem. Immediately following the lawnmower distance record attempt in front of the high school students, I raised the lawnmower above my head in celebration. That wouldn't have been a problem but when I set it back down, it hit the ground hard and the axle popped out. I worried I might have to quickly find a new lawnmower, which was what took me the most time initially. Thankfully, I was able to pop it back in making this next record attempt possible. Balancing while standing still is a skill that leverages the same talent and muscle set as balancing while walking but requires less movement while also requiring a greater pain tolerance.

The previous year, the Cradlepoint partner conference took place the week my first son was born. A year later we had our next partner conference. I was developing a reputation as "the juggler" and now Guinness World Records title breaker among the wider Cradlepoint community. I was asked if I was interested in setting a Guinness World Records title as part of the partner conference activities. I jumped at the chance. I didn't have a ton of time to prepare, but I had been spending time building up my neck strength to walk 200 meters with a lawnmower on my chin. The sister record for distance walked was for the longest duration balancing a lawnmower on my chin. I decided to go for it.

The final conference dinner was held at JUMP – Jack's Urban Meeting Place, a multi-purpose center with spaces for people and groups to get together and explore ideas, named after Jack Simplot of Idaho potato fame. The event was held on the sixth floor overlooking beautiful downtown Boise. I gave a short talk explaining why I break records and the power of having a growth mindset. I then placed the 23-pound lawnmower on my chin, held it with my hands for a few seconds, and released.

The previous record of 5 minutes 1 second was announced and displayed above me on a projector screen as the mark to beat alongside a stopwatch marking my progress. As the stopwatch on the screen crossed the one-minute mark, there were scattered shouts of encouragement and probably just as many shushes for them to be quiet. I made it past two minutes and then my neck really started to hurt. Two and a half minutes in my jaw started locking up. I flexed and bent my knees to increase blood flow and tried to ignore the pain in my jaw. I was wearing a Cradlepoint polo shirt with a blazer. At three minutes I started sweating. I tried to steady my breathing and focus on the top of the lawnmower to block out the pain that was shooting through my body from overexertion and muscle fatigue. When I passed four minutes, my confidence was high, but I still had a minute of pain to endure. As I approached five minutes, the pain was intense.

If it were a practice session, I would have stopped. In fact, I had been in much less pain during several practice sessions and stopped several times. But each time I practiced, I tried to go a little longer and push through a little more pain. At first 20-30 seconds was all I could handle. But then I could go a minute, then two, then three. I had to build up the muscle strength, so the pain wasn't quite as intense, but that required putting myself through even more pain. I finally got strong enough that I knew I could break the record if I could push through the pain.

Today, I was going to push through. There was no way I was going to give up. As the clock ticked past five minutes, I raised my hands in celebration. I kept them out to the side to make it clear my hands weren't going to touch the mower and end the attempt. At that point, the audience began to cheer, and I had a moment of elation. I decided to get clever and, while keeping the lawnmower balanced on my chin, I unbuttoned my blazer and swiftly took it off, letting it fall to the floor. I was sweating so profusely at this point I grabbed the front bottom of my shirt and waved it in and out to cool off. I wanted to balance the lawnmower longer, but the pain was overwhelming. I didn't feel like I was doing any permanent damage to my body, but once I reached 5 minutes 30 seconds, the will to keep pushing was sapped. I had broken the record and that was enough. Once I lost the will to continue, I stopped. If the existing record had been for a longer length of time, I have no doubt I could have persevered far beyond the five and a half minutes. I pulled the lawnmower off my chin knowing the hard work had paid off. The pain would subside, but the victory would last. Sometimes success requires simply hanging on and powering through.

Longest Duration Balancing a Lawnmower on the Chin
Previous Record: 5 minutes 1 second
New Record: 5 minutes 31 seconds

20
SETTING SMART GOALS

Most Juggling Catches in 1 Minute Blindfolded (3 Balls)
Previous Record: 363 catches (held by me)

There was one record on my list I wanted to break more than any other. I was the current record holder for the fastest blindfolded juggling in the world, but I had missed my chance to break it again on live national television. Moreover, I wanted to not only break it but also break the record for the world's fastest juggling at the same time.

I had failed before, but failure is simply an opportunity to improve. Failure is learning in progress. Failure only becomes a failure when you end there. Failure does not define you, how you respond to it does. One of the best ways to reach your goals is to set goals, and SMART ones at that. First, you need goals. If you don't know where you want to go, it's hard to get there. You don't always have to have the end in sight, but you can set interim goals to keep progressing. For example, you may not know what you want to be doing in five years, but you know what you're doing now, and you can set a short-term goal.

I have a long-term goal of breaking the Guinness World Records title for the longest duration juggling three bowling balls. To break it, I'll have to juggle three ten-pound bowling balls for over a minute. I may be over a year away from building up the strength to break that record. A short-term goal could be to go to the gym three times this next week. When I get to the gym, I like to set goals for the number of sets for each exercise and the numbers of reps for each set. When I pick up two 20-pound weights, I say to myself: I want to complete 80 reps in each hand in the next minute. I have long term goals and short-term goals.

To be effective, goals should be SMART: Specific, Measurable,

Attainable, Realistic, and Timely. To start, the goal should be specific. If all you say is "I want to better myself," "I want to have a good career," or "I want to get in shape," what are you working toward? If instead, you say, "I want to run a sub-nine-minute mile" or "I want to make associate manager by age 35," you have specific tangible goals you can work towards. My goal was to break the blindfolded speed juggling record and simultaneously break the overall speed juggling record.

The goal should be measurable. That's how you know if or when you've reached it. "I want to run a fast mile" isn't measurable. If instead you say, "I want to run a sub-nine-minute mile," it becomes measurable. You know when you've achieved it. I had to get 363 catches in one minute to break the blindfolded speed juggling record and 428 catches to match the overall speed juggling record.

Goals should be attainable. You should have the ability to reach your goal. A significant part of the message I try to impart on those I get to meet is that most people have more ability than they think they do, so I suggest stretching your comfort zone when setting an attainable goal. If you say you want to fly like superman without any equipment, your goal isn't attainable. If you are five feet two inches tall and 35 years old and your goal is to become six feet six inches tall, you had better reevaluate. But if you're 35, stuck in a dead-end career, and you say you've always wanted to become a lawyer, you have an attainable goal if you're willing to put in the years of effort required to pursue that dream.

The goal should also be realistic; it should fit within the hierarchy of priorities in your life. Maybe a goal is attainable, but if you're not willing or able to put in the time and effort to achieve it, it's not realistic. Maybe you want to play in the NBA, but the time and effort required to gain NBA-level basketball skills aren't something you're willing to put in (hours per day for years). There are certainly those not born with physical gifts that still reach the pinnacle of their sport. Stephen Curry of the NBA Golden State Warriors doesn't have the physical traits usually associated with elite basketball players. He was undersized, not especially fast or strong, and he only received modest recruiting attention in high school and college. He used what he had and worked hard at every stage to become the best he could be. Because he wasn't "gifted," during his back-to-back 2015-2016 MVP seasons, he was so underpaid he was the sixth highest-paid player on his own team! He was the 79th highest-paid player in the NBA, but he did go on to become the highest-paid player in the league. I love his underdog story, his work ethic, and his circus-like three-point shots. For this reason, he is one of my favorite athletes.

The goals should also be timely. This means it should have a deadline. It shouldn't be a vague "I'll do this in the future." I want to run a sub-six-minute mile isn't quite specific enough. If you don't have a deadline, it's hard to stay motivated to work toward your goal or practice. It allows you to procrastinate. If there isn't a deadline, it lacks urgency, so you can put it off until later. You should pick an end. It could be something like I want to be able to do 100 consecutive pushups by the start of summer, I will apply to the management training program before my second work anniversary, or I will finish writing a book by October 15th of this year. That way you must act now to meet your goal.

The time and effort required to break a Guinness World Records title don't fit within most people's other important goals like getting in shape, having a successful career, or being a devoted parent and spouse. It certainly could fit within yours if you wanted it to, so the difference between a goal being realistic or not is often tied directly to your mindset. If you have a growth mindset and are willing to put blood, sweat, and tears into pursuing your passion, myriad previously unrealistic goals become realistic.

I had one such unrealistic goal, that became realistic when I pursued it with a growth mindset. I wanted to become the fastest juggler in the world, and I wanted to do it while blindfolded. I had failed, succeeded, and failed again at breaking the blindfolded speed juggling record. The most recent failure was my most spectacular one on the TODAY show and aired live for an audience of 5 million people and was seen by all my family and friends. That painful memory was still fresh in my mind, and to overcome that failure I wanted to not just break the record, but also to redeem myself. I didn't just want to break the blindfolded speed juggling record, I wanted to show the world I could break the overall speed juggling record while blindfolded. An opportunity to do just that presented itself in May of 2017.

At the inaugural FIRST Robotics Idaho Regional in Boise, Don Bossi, the president of the organization, saw me give a STEM talk replete with juggling, inspiration, and a successful Guinness World Records title attempt. He offered me an open invitation to the FIRST Robotics National Championship to speak and possibly break a record. I thought an event with 40,000 people would be a good place to go big. I worked with the conference director to line up a speaking slot as part of the optional conference series with my presentation scheduled in an auditorium in St Louis that seated a thousand people. I also worked with her to organize my next Guinness World Records title attempt later that same day for the most selfies taken in one hour (all with different people). That story comes in the next chapter.

I set a goal of breaking the blindfold speed juggling record during the FIRST National Championship in St. Louis with a stretch goal of breaking the overall speed juggling world record at the same time. The goal was specific: break a particular world record; measurable: 363 and 428 juggling catches in one minute; attainable: I knew I could do it; realistic: I had enough time and motivation to practice, and timely: I had a deadline.

My wife, one-year-old son, and I flew out to St. Louis and rented an Airbnb near the conference held in the NFL St. Louis Rams' former stadium. I coordinated with the event to have volunteers lined up for timing, witnessing, and videoing the attempt, but when I checked with the volunteer coordinators the day before, they had no record of any volunteers for my event.

On the morning of the attempt, I showed up early to the theater. Since I didn't have prearranged volunteers, I pulled a few people from the audience who had also shown up early and asked if they would act as timers and witnesses.

I told the students how I became an engineer and how I met my wife at MIT where she was also studying to become an engineer. She had participated in FIRST Robotics in high school, and it inspired her to pursue Mechanical Engineering. Without that FIRST Robotics experience, Jennifer probably wouldn't have gone to MIT, and we would never have met. I thought it was one of the best talks I'd given, which made me happy as I had spent a significant amount of time preparing, writing, rehearsing, and polishing it. I was a little disappointed that less than 100 people showed up to an auditorium that held a thousand at an event with 40,000 attendees. I decided to make the most of it, and we all had a good time.

I left plenty of time before the end of the conference talk timeslot to make the record attempt. I knew I might get nervous and drop the ball a few times, so I wanted plenty of time for several attempts. Extra attempt flexibility serves two purposes: one is that I have several attempts to break the record, and the other is that since I know I have lots of attempts, I feel less pressure. With less pressure, I get less nervous and am more likely to break the record on one of the first attempts.

The newly recruited timers and witnesses were all briefed before the show and joined me on stage for the record attempt. I explained to the audience that the blindfold speed juggling record was 363 catches and the overall speed juggling record was 428. We had one practice "ready, set, go" in front of the entire audience. Then we did it for real. On the first attempt, I had a solid run and juggled for 54 seconds before I dropped a ball. I got 410 catches and broke the blindfolded speed juggling record on the first try.

We couldn't decide if we should celebrate or be disappointed. The audience and I did a little math and realized I was on pace for 450 catches if I had continued juggling for the last 6 seconds. They knew both the blindfolded speed juggling record and the overall juggling record and if they could witness me becoming the fastest juggler in the world, period, while blindfolded, they wanted to see it. I had to try again. On the second try I got more nervous which decreased my juggling pace. I juggled for 59 seconds before dropping a ball. I got 426 catches. I was so close I could taste it. I had more adrenaline in my system this time and the nerves caused me to juggle more erratically and thus slower, especially after the 300-catch mark. I had never been so close to my goal on a live record attempt without making it. I tried again and juggled for only six seconds this time with too much adrenaline coursing through my veins. I tried again and made another 54-second run. I let out a grating "Come, on! I'm getting so close!" The audience clapped in encouragement.

I took a break to give a short and pointed motivational speech about how when things don't go your way, you don't give up. I told them point-blank, I was going to keep going at this until I got it. A few had other places to be and departed, and I didn't hold it against them. Then I had a 29-second run. I started on the next one immediately and made it 15 seconds. I then got yet another 54-second run before adrenaline rendered my arms unable to continue. On the next run, I got nervous but was able to hold it together for over 59 seconds. It wasn't my fastest run of the day, but I still missed the last catch that would have gotten me 429 catches. The next time, I didn't get nervous, but after 51 seconds made a mistake. With a calm voice I told the audience that I didn't get nervous that time, I just dropped a ball.

I tried again. This time I said, "I feel it this time, we're getting really close." I juggled for 52 seconds before making a mistake. I let out an audible exhale with my lips pursed. I didn't say a word. After a few seconds, the audience broke out in applause. I said, "You can see where I'm struggling." At about 50 seconds, I hit the physiological barrier. I started again. I bobbled the juggling balls and recovered, I bobbled again and recovered again. After 50 seconds, I could juggle no more.

I did another practice run and asked the group "How are we doing on time?" I walked to the lectern and checked the time on my phone. We'd been at it for quite some time but still had time left in the hour. "Here we go." Less than 30 seconds later I dropped a ball. "I'm trying to go faster in the front... so I'll have more time at the end." The pattern started to fall apart near the end of the next attempt. I tried to keep it together, but after 51 seconds a ball from my right hand went long and sailed over my left hand. I let out a whooshing distressed "whoooo!" I had been on stage for over an hour. "A couple more tries here. I'm feeling it. I'm feeling it." The audience let me know they were there to support me. I was appreciative. I started again, counting every third catch out loud into my lapel mic like I did every juggling run. I made it 27 seconds and dropped a ball. Under my breath, I uttered a "Come on," picked up the ball and started again immediately. I counted to 50, then 50 again for 300 catches. I kept going and this time I counted up to 46 again before the timer called out "Stop!" indicating the full minute had elapsed. I lifted the blindfold off my eyes, jumped into the air, and let out a bellowing "COME ON! YES! Folks, What Just Happened?!" as they cheered and clapped. They had stuck with me for over an hour and five minutes. Painful drop after painful drop they stuck around as I stuck with it. I was now the fastest juggler in the world, and I set the mark while blindfolded. At the end of the last run, I was so nervous I had to push the lump in my throat down and keep the butterflies in my stomach from fluttering up.

I wanted my excitement to transfer to the kids in a meaningful way, so I launched into my closing monologue with vigor. "I didn't just become the world's fastest blindfolded juggler, I just became the world's fastest juggler. Period. While blindfolded! And that's what I want you to be able to do. I don't mean juggling. I want you to leave here today believing you could win nationals in autonomous mode. I want you to make self-driving cars a reality. Make them not just three times safer than they are today. Make them not just 10 times safer, but a hundred, a thousand times safer. Get rid of accidents. Help us go to Mars and make humans an interplanetary species. Then figure out sustainable energy. That's not a political statement; that's a tautological statement. To use energy long-term, it has to be sustainable."

After they were dismissed, I gathered the witnesses around the computer to play the video back in slow motion. The video review of the evidence revealed that my live count was incorrect. I didn't beat the all-time speed juggling record, I tied it with 428 catches which was still good enough.

My goal was complete. It met all the criteria of a SMART goal and I practiced, prepared, and executed before my deadline. I almost failed to achieve my stretch goal, but I just eked it out. That was good enough for me. I will likely revisit this record in the future. Perhaps someone else will break it first, or I'll want to challenge my own mark. But whenever that time comes, I'll be sure to set it as a goal of mine and I'll make it a SMART goal to ensure I have a specific target in mind, a chance to break it, and can do it in a timely manner.

Most Juggling Catches in 1 Minute Blindfolded (3 Balls)
Previous Record: 363 catches (held by me)
New Record: 428 catches (tied most juggling catches in one minute with the eyes open)

21
PRACTICE VISUALIZING

Most Self-Portrait Photographs (Selfies) Taken in 1 Hour
Previous Record: 1,449 selfies

I went to the St. Louis FIRST Championships planning to erase my blindfolded speed juggling defeat and decided I wanted to go for the biggest record attempt I'd ever made. Since the event would host nearly 40,000 people, it was the perfect opportunity to break a record that would require more audience participation than any record I had ever tried: the most selfies taken in one hour. The person breaking the record has to take all the pictures with other people in them, and each other person is only allowed to appear in one selfie. Both peoples' entire faces need to be in the shot, and they have to be recognizable. The previous record of 1,449 selfies was daunting but doable. I'd need to take one selfie with a different person every 2.5 seconds.

I spent a few months getting ready. I was practicing for the record of most selfies in 3 minutes already, and my strategy of having a line approaching me from either side was well-rehearsed. I had one practice with nearly 100 people and an official attempt with 128 selfies under my belt. The official 128 selfie effort had been disqualified since my timers' faces were visible in the background and showed up in multiple pictures invalidating all but the first picture they showed up in. I also practiced with balloons taped to the wall on either side of me to simulate heads and another further out on each side to simulate another person standing nearby as if they were the next in line. I needed to be sure to capture the closer balloon in its entirety and none of the next balloon. After several practices, I was getting better but needed more practice. I didn't always have a camera or balloons to practice. So instead, I practiced in my head.

In *Mindset*, Carol Dweck references a study of basketball players practicing free-throws. Researchers brought both beginner and intermediate basketball players in for the study. The researchers had all the players shoot free throws to get a baseline measurement of how good they were at the start. The researchers then tasked the beginner and intermediate players to practice a specified number of free throws each day. They were randomly assigned to practice in one of two ways. Some practiced actual free throws while others only visualized practicing the same number of free throws. A control group didn't practice at all. The researchers brought the subjects back at the end of the study to measure their improvement. What the researchers found was that the intermediate basketball players who practiced improved. It didn't matter whether they took actual free throws or only practiced by visualizing taking free throws, they both improved by similar amounts. Intermediate players who didn't practice did not improve. Among beginners, those who practiced actual free throws improved the most while those who didn't practice or only visualized taking free throws didn't improve much at all. This suggests that once you know what you're supposed to do, thinking about it and visualizing it in detail can help you improve. What you're doing during visualization or physical practice is solidifying the right behaviors by strengthening the neural pathways in your brain that already exist by thinking through them again. If you don't know what you're doing yet, thinking about it may not be helpful since you can't think in vivid detail what you're supposed to be doing. If you want to improve at something, you may not always be able to physically practice. But once you know what you're supposed to do, it's possible to improve just by thinking through it in detail.

Using this visualization technique, I was able to prepare for taking an hour's worth of selfies by mentally rehearsing what I would do during that hour with all the possible situations I could plausibly imagine happening. What would happen if I had multiple tall people on either side of me? What if the lines alternated with short and tall people? What if there were a person in a wheelchair or an empty line on one side? How would I hold the camera when my arms became fatigued? And how could I still take pictures if I couldn't hold my arms out anymore? I sorted through these issues and more by clearly visualizing each scenario in my head and determining the appropriate reaction. I had the real-world experience to draw upon with one 100-person practice, one 128-person Guinness World Records title attempt, and even more practices with balloons. Since I had a baseline to start with, the visualized practice helped me improve dramatically.

The key to making visualization effective is to make it as real as possible. You need to put yourself in the situation, see yourself there, feel yourself there, make the sights, sounds, and emotions as clear as you can in your head. I suspect the beginner basketball players didn't improve as much while visualizing because they weren't able to make it as real as possible. They didn't have the right mechanics to visualize since they didn't have real memories to rely on during their visualizations.

If you want to practice for a board presentation, you should envision the room, the setup, the board members in their chairs. Let yourself feel what you'll feel the day of the presentation. You may be nervous and want to act confident. Let yourself experience those emotions as you visualize the experience. The physical process that's happening in the brain when you're visualizing a situation is very similar to the one that happens in real life. The same neurons are being fired, and the same neural pathways are being strengthened.

I thought about how I would lean back and forth left and right as my legs supported my shifting weight. I feigned the muscle fatigue and thought about how it would affect my physical form as the hour wore on. I wouldn't be able to bend my knees as deep, or I'd get muscle cramps in my quads. I feared arm fatigue since the camera that worked best to quickly and reliably take in-focus pictures weighed a full three pounds. I eliminated taking a step to the right and left by angling the camera to the right and left. The extra step not only took extra time, but it increased the likelihood of either a collision with the incoming person or leaving too large a gap between us.

I also considered other execution options like lining up with a lot of different people in one shot and having them all hold cardboard squares over their faces until it was time for their selfie. I decided the complexity of the operation and training involved was too risky, so I abandoned that approach.

I coordinated with the FIRST event hosts and set a date and time for the selfie attempt. I asked for 20-30 volunteers to help direct traffic, get folks signed in (a dozen at a time), and ensure we had a steady flow of people. When I showed up at the event, six-foot-tall signs were announcing the selfie attempt in the hallway between venues. The problem was the hallway wasn't wide enough to hold the lines, take pictures, and have folks sign the roster while still allowing for normal traffic flow.

I talked to the organizers, and we decided to move the attempt inside the lunch hall. The lighting wasn't as good in the lunchroom, increasing the risk of blurred photos since the exposure time would need to be longer for each photo. There also wasn't a wall in the main lighted area of the lunchroom, so I needed drapes set up to prevent folks in the background from showing up in the pictures. I had one of the six-foot signs advertising the event moved into the lunchroom to advertise where the Guinness World Records attempt would take place for anyone passing by to see. What I didn't realize was the lunchroom that sat several hundred people would not have hundreds of people in it during lunch, even with thousands of people attending the competition. It turned out there were many other more popular lunch options.

On the morning of the attempt, I gave a talk and juggling show where I broke the blindfolded speed juggling record. The plan was to advertise to the hundreds of people in the thousand-person auditorium and get them so excited about seeing a Guinness World Records title attempt that they would want to be part of one. Unfortunately, there were less than 100 people in attendance. Additionally, the night before at the opening ceremonies, I wandered around the stadium filled with tens of thousands of people and made announcements to any group that would listen that they could take part in a Guinness World Records title attempt the next day. I was feeling alright about the attempt. Physically, I was ready; mentally, I was prepared; I just needed enough people willing to take selfies with me.

A few minutes before the attempt was supposed to start, I briefed the ten volunteers who were there. It wasn't as many as I hoped, so I assigned limited roles with the line control folks giving instructions for people to go one at a time and not cover their faces. I had a couple of girls hand out stickers to let participants know where they could find their selfies online, and others were to ensure everyone signed in. At this point, I was getting worried for two reasons. One was that I had no witnesses. The record wouldn't be official without at least two adult witnesses who could stay the entire hour. The volunteer coordinators were trying to find someone but weren't having much luck. The second reason I was worried is that the lunchroom only had about 50 of the 500 chairs occupied, and there were not many people passing through the area. I told all the volunteers that if we got low on people in the lines, pretty much everyone needed to abandon their posts and go find more people. If there weren't enough people, it would all be for naught.

A couple of minutes after the planned start time, the volunteer coordinator had rounded up two not particularly enthusiastic, but still, willing volunteers to act as witnesses for the hour. That was good enough for me since we needed to get started.

I taped arrows on the floor for the lines of people to follow, and we started getting folks lined up for the start of the attempt. When we were ready to go, there were only about 100 people in line. I could take selfies with that many in less than two minutes if I was moving fast but only needed to keep up half that pace for the hour to break the current record. I started the video cameras and after a "ready, set, go," we started.

I took a picture with the person on my right side and pivoted to the left, then back to the right, back and forth, left and right. For the first couple of minutes, the people flew by almost as fast as the time. I was swift but deliberate. I knew we may be tight on the number of participants required to break the record, so I made sure every selfie would count with the face exposed, fully in frame, and in focus. I also directed people forward and told them to make sure to sign the roster. I was planning to have the volunteers manage that, but I figured I had the extra time and didn't want to take enough selfies only to find out the Guinness World Records-required roster was incomplete. There was a swarm of people around the sign-in table filling out the dozen roster forms for the first few minutes. After about five minutes, both lines of people were depleted.

It was time for the volunteers to abandon their stations to recruit more people. Some went to the hallways to pull in any people walking by. Others went around to all the lunch tables to ensure everyone had their photo taken. On either side of the lunchroom were bullpens of people with robot demos and robot playing fields. Some volunteers were good at grabbing anyone they could find. Not only did they point them where to go but they also escorted them back. For the next 20 minutes, someone was always getting a photo taken or on his or her way toward me to get his or her photo taken. I'd take the shot and direct them to the sign-in table. About halfway through the hour, there was a pause with every person within visual range ineligible to have their picture taken again. There was no one in line and no one coming towards us. The pause only lasted a few seconds, and another group of people came in. The pauses started happening more and more frequently. Sometimes it was a single person that would come, sometimes a family, and sometimes an entire robotics team that could keep me busy taking selfies for a while. Most of the time I was only taking pictures on one side since all the people in a group would arrive together and not realize there were supposed to be two lines for faster processing.

About 45 minutes into the hour, the pauses got longer. There were no more groups of readily available people nearby. Many of the robotics team members in the large bullpen adjacent to the lunchroom were assigned to their posts and couldn't leave until they were relieved by someone else. At one point, during a pause of thirty seconds, I took the moment to check that the photos I was taking were turning out in focus, sufficiently lit, and only had a single face. The ones I looked at were all good.

I felt busy, but I wasn't sure we were going fast enough. I had printed off little stickers to hand out to everyone after they got their selfies taken. If everything went perfectly, I figured I could get 3,600 selfies (one per second). I knew that wouldn't happen, so I only printed off 3,000 stickers. That was over twice as many as I would need to break the record. If I was only moving at half speed and made sure they all counted, we could still break the record.

As time wound down, trickles of people kept coming, and we took a few more pictures. The one-minute warning was called out, and a few more people showed up. With the last 10 seconds winding down, a couple more people showed up, I called them to hurry, and we snapped their selfies just as time expired.

At the end of the hour, I felt relief but also excitement and anticipation mixed with anxiety. Had I broken the record? I was well short of the 3,000 people I thought I could get since there were lots of pauses, but I only needed to get half that many. I wondered if the gaps were too long.

I shut off the video cameras and booted up my computer to transfer all the selfies, so the witnesses and I could count and verify them. A few of the volunteers were excitedly hovering nearby. I estimated I had taken between 1,300 and 1,700 selfies. If I fell within that estimated range, I thought I had a 50/50 chance I'd broken the record.

Several of the more active and excited volunteers gathered to look over my shoulder as I began transferring photos from the SD card to the computer. They had just spent a frantic hour grabbing anyone they could find to participate in a Guinness World Records title attempt. These kids loved Guinness World Records and were thrilled to be part of an official attempt. Their efforts were in the hope that they could not only have their selfie as part of the attempt but also play a pivotal role in making the record attempt a success.

I opened the folder and selected the photos and began copying them onto my computer desktop. I looked at the file count and it was only 600 hundred images; nowhere near the 1,449 needed to break the record. I was sure I'd taken way more than that, so I tried to figure out what had happened. I realized the last image was titled DSC_9999. When my camera reaches 10,000 images, it rolls back over to start at DSC_0001 in a new folder. I found the other folder, selected those images, and began copying. I knew we were going to have to discard several as duplicates and others where both faces were not fully in frame. I was hoping to see well north of 1,500 total images and wanted closer to 1,600 to ensure we'd have enough after duplicates and non-qualifying images were discarded. I had prepped the team that it might take another hour to validate the photos and get the official selfie count. After copying the second folder of images onto my computer, the total count of all the selfies taken from both folders before we subtracted the disqualifications was 930.

I was in disbelief. Was there another folder I was missing? Where were the rest of the pictures? All the pauses without people and the realization that I had time to tell everyone to sign the roster hit me. The theoretical max of 3,600 was misleading since that required perfection and speed, and a steady but fast pace was still required to even reach half that number. My pace was neither steady nor fast. I wasn't even close.

I thanked the team and let the witnesses know that they didn't have to stick around to validate the selfies since we didn't break the record. All I needed was some help peeling the tape off the ground as part of the cleanup. As I reached down to peel trampled tape off the ground, I realized it's a lot less fun to clean up after a failure. But doing what is necessary, even after a setback, and not giving up is fundamental to long term success.

Instead of hiding my failure and acting like it didn't happen, I decided to embrace it. I had Jennifer, my wife, put all the selfies in consolidated images with 30 selfies per page and posted them to my website and Facebook page for folks to come to find, tag, and read about the attempt, even if we didn't break the Guinness World Record. I did still have a major success that day breaking the blindfolded speed juggling record, but I also had a major setback. I still plan to try again someday to break this record. I learned a lot during this attempt that will set me up for success on my next attempt. Instead of viewing this as a failure, I'll consider it my first full-scale practice run. When I go to practice it again, I'll have even more knowledge to draw from when I visualize the event during my practice time. I'm no longer a novice selfie taker, and visualization will be key to my next success.

Most Self-Portrait Photographs (Selfies) Taken in 1 Hour
Previous Record: 1,449 selfies
My Attempt: 908 selfies

EPILOGUE

I find it appropriate to end this book on a failed record attempt. This book is as much about failure as it is about success. Almost every success was preceded by hundreds or even thousands of failures. I practiced, failed, tried again, and failed again. I kept trying until I felt I could succeed in front of a live audience. Many times, I did succeed, but several times, I did not. In our lives, it is not our failures that define us but how we respond to them. We don't remember Abraham Lincoln for his failures, of which he had many. We focus only on his final successes as President. I didn't give up after this spectacular most selfies in one-hour failure. I put in significant time, energy, and effort - not to speak of the cost of travel for this event, but I didn't let this setback deter me from pressing on. I learned from this failure and others and used them as opportunities to improve myself.

I also don't want to give the impression that I was able to accomplish what I have in life by myself. I have family, friends, mentors, witnesses, timers, and acquaintances that have helped me every step of the way. My wife Jennifer has been my best and most supportive partner and without her support, I would have had nowhere near the success I have had to date. Be sure to reach out for help to those you know and some you may not yet know when you get stuck or could use a hand. And not only is it important to just ask for help and have family and friends, but you also need to cultivate your community. You need to reach out and make friends. You need to show appreciation (and mean it!) for all the help you get in life because none of us could have gotten to where we are without those around us.

I have now gone on to break over 150 Guinness World Records titles including greatest distance traveled on foot while juggling blindfolded (100 yards and recently over a third of a mile), most peas eaten in 30 seconds with a cocktail stick/toothpick (49), and greatest distance and longest time balancing a pool cue on one finger while walking (20 miles and 4 hours 20 minutes). I juggled three 3-pound axes for 839 consecutive catches and three 10-pound bowling balls for 30 seconds. I took 164 bites out of 3 apples in one minute while juggling them. I stuck 100 candles in my mouth and lit them on fire for 30 seconds. I sliced 62 kiwis in half with a samurai sword while standing balanced on a swiss exercise ball. I identified 11 different flavors of ice cream in one minute while blindfolded. I skipped a half marathon in 2 hours 14 minutes 41.8 seconds. I made 220 juggling catches of 3 basketballs in one minute. I ran a 7-minute 54-second mile while juggling 3 balls while blindfolded. I have pushed myself to my physical and mental limits and by doing so have increased those limits. When you say you can't do something, it is an artificial restraint you place on yourself. The more you remove those constraints by having a growth mindset, the more you can grow.

This book is more than just a list of things to do or a set of steps to reach your goals; it's practical advice to get there. My recommendation is not to try to apply all 21 things at once but rather pick the lessons that make the most sense to you. Pick the ones that motivate you and that resonate with you. Pick the ones you'll stick with. But if there's one that is absolutely critical to success, it's having a growth mindset. It's having the belief that if you follow some of these pieces of advice, that your life can indeed change. You can get better. You can get smarter. You can change things about yourself that you may have long thought were set in stone if you work hard enough at it. Stop telling yourself you can't dance and take a dance lesson. Stop saying you're bad at math and try harder and work smarter in the next class. Don't say you can't remember peoples' names, instead learn the techniques that allow you to more easily remember them. The apple doesn't fall far from the tree is only an aphorism for people who think that way. You may have been told by someone with a fixed mindset that you're not smart, that you're not athletic, or that only a very small percentage of people go on to be successful, but I guarantee you that if you believe you can be successful at whatever it is you're trying to do, you're taking the first step to get there. And once you've taken the first step you've started, and that's half the battle. All that is left is to finish. Enjoy the journey.

The End